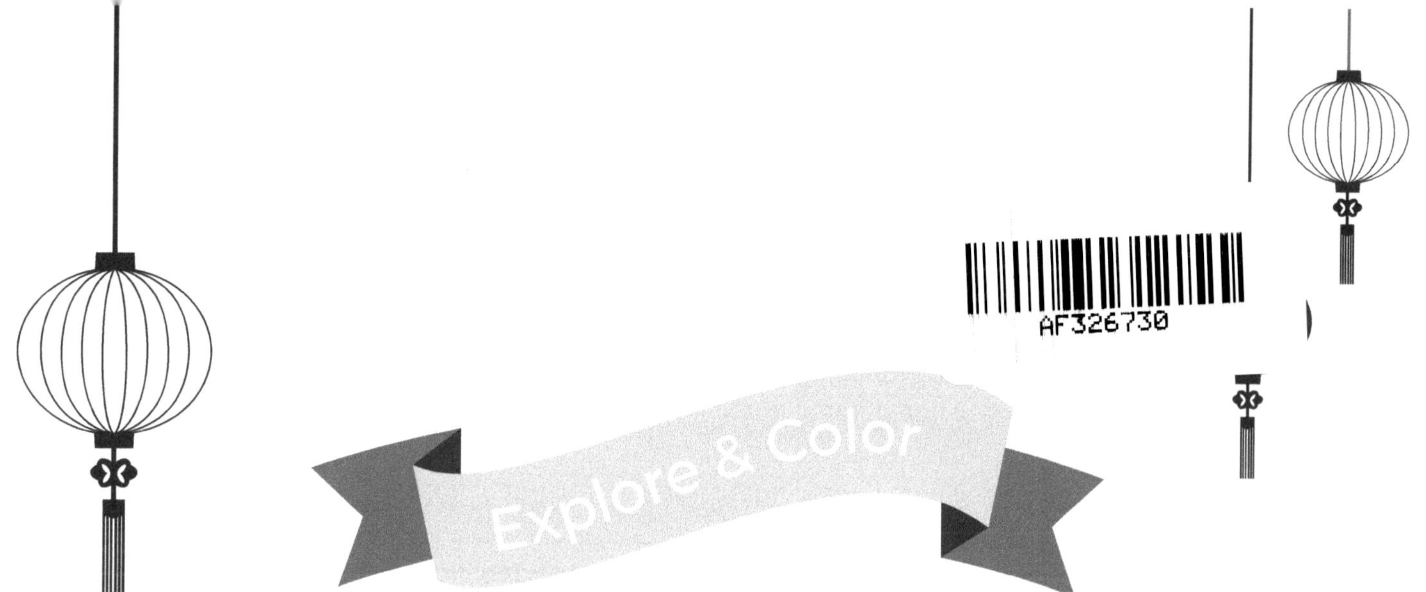

San Francisco

CHINATOWN

Coloring Book & Cultural Guide

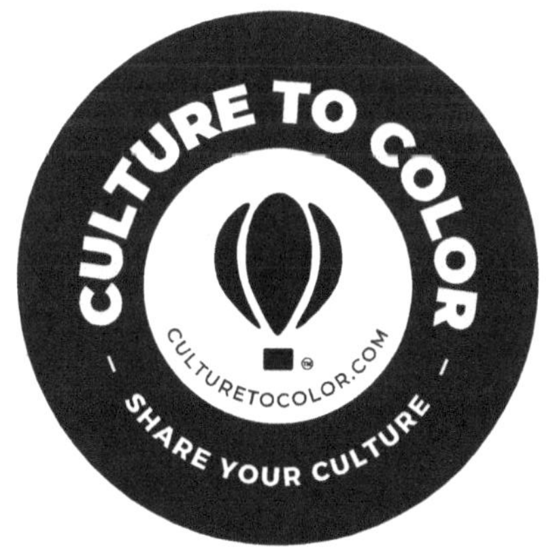

Bibi LeBlanc

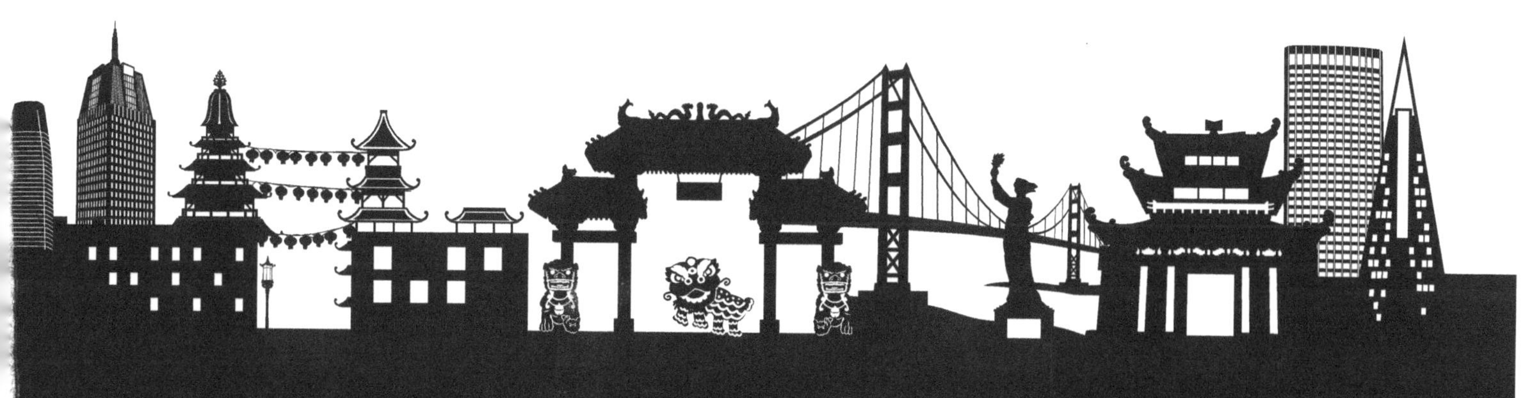

Published by

Culture to Color, LLC

CS@CultureToColor.com

USA: 386-228-5147

By best-selling author and Gold Medal winner of the FAPA President's Book Award

and a finalist in the Eric Hoffer International Book Award for her book

Explore the Sights of Berlin Divided—Berlin United/Berlin Geteilt—Berlin Vereint.

Gold Award winner of the Kops-Fetherling International Book

Award for *Discover Food & Wine of Tuscany.*

Purple Dragonfly International Book Award, International Book Award,

IBPA Benjamin Franklin Book Award, and Silver Medal winner of the FAPA

President's Book Award for *Endangered Animals of North America.*

Next Generation International Indie Book Award, Purple Dragonfly

International Book Award, FAPA President's Book Award, and NYC Big

Book Award for *Explore the Sights of San Francisco, Chinatown*

Cover Design & Interior by: Nicole Neese

Asst. Designer: Ginger Marks, DocUmeant Designs

Printed in the USA

First Edition

10 9 8 7 6 5 4 3 2

ISBN: 9781733798532

To order in bulk contact publisher at CultureToColor.com

For more information visit: **CultureToColor.com**

Contents

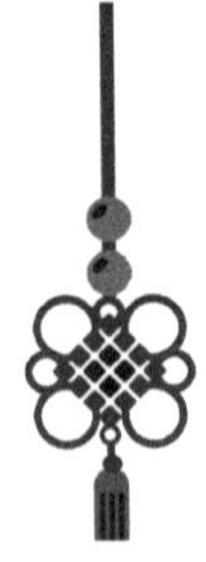

WELCOME TO SAN FRANCISCO CHINATOWN
旧金山中国城欢迎您

"People shape places, and places shape people."
— Frank Wong in Forever, Chinatown, a cultural/historical documentary

Whether you are here for one of the spectacular celebrations or just happened upon Chinatown, you will immediately be drawn in by the colors, sights, smells, and sounds of San Francisco's most unique neighborhood!

A LITTLE BIT OF HISTORY

Chinatown has a rich and fascinating history. Early Chinese settlers came in search of a better life and found work in the gold mines and on the railroad. Later arrivals on the West Coast found themselves forbidden to enter the country and interned on Angel Island in the San Francisco Bay. Eventually, restrictions were eased, and a vibrant Chinese community began to develop. The enclave grew around Portsmouth Square, the city's first public square, establishing the needed amenities: stores, schools, associations, newspapers, recreation, and places of worship.

After the 1906 earthquake and fires destroyed Chinatown, local authorities attempted to relocate it to the city's outskirts. Community leaders quickly started rebuilding the neighborhood in a distinctive Chinese style to attract outside visitors and succeeded in convincing city officials to keep Chinatown in its original location.

If you are interested in the history of this vibrant community and would like to delve deeper, take a tour with a local guide and/or visit the *Chinese Historical Society of America*. The *CHSA* is a museum and cultural center at 965 Clay Street that displays exhibits chronicling the experience of the Chinese in San Francisco. Frank Wong's *Memories in Miniatures* is a must-see addition to the museum's collection!

TODAY

Chinatown is a city within the city of San Francisco. Though there are many Chinatowns around the globe, this one is the oldest and largest outside of China. One of the most popular attractions in San Francisco, this dynamic community attracts millions of visitors each year.

READY TO EXPLORE

One of the main draws of Chinatown is the diversity of things to do, see, and experience. The Dragon Gate, Chinatown's southern entrance and excellent photo-op, is a great place to start your exploration. Beyond the gate, you will find yourself on Grant Avenue, lined with dragon streetlamps, eclectic shops, and a variety of restaurants. From here, just follow your senses and let the intriguing sights of gilded balconies, pagoda rooftops, and alluring aromas from a bakery or the smell of incense lead you off the beaten path. Wander down a narrow alley and into an herb store, temple, or market — this celebrated neighborhood is truly a feast for the senses … and even more so, if you are in town during one of the spectacular events such as the New Year celebration, Spring Festival, or Autumn Moon Festival!

WORKED UP AN APPETITE

From dim sum and pastries to roast ducks you'll see hanging in restaurant windows on Stockton Street, there is a unique variety of food and restaurants to choose from in Chinatown. Whatever you do, don't leave without sampling the local cuisine!

Chinatown is continuously changing and evolving. Whether you get the chance to explore it in person or right here on paper with coloring pens in hand — it is a fascinating place to visit and a cultural experience you don't want to miss!

What are some of the things to see and experience in Chinatown? Step in and discover for yourself in the pages that follow …

HAPPY COLORING,

Bibi

AWARD-WINNING AUTHOR & FOUNDER
CULTURE TO COLOR

P.S. I would love to hear from you. You can reach me at bibi@culturetocolor.com

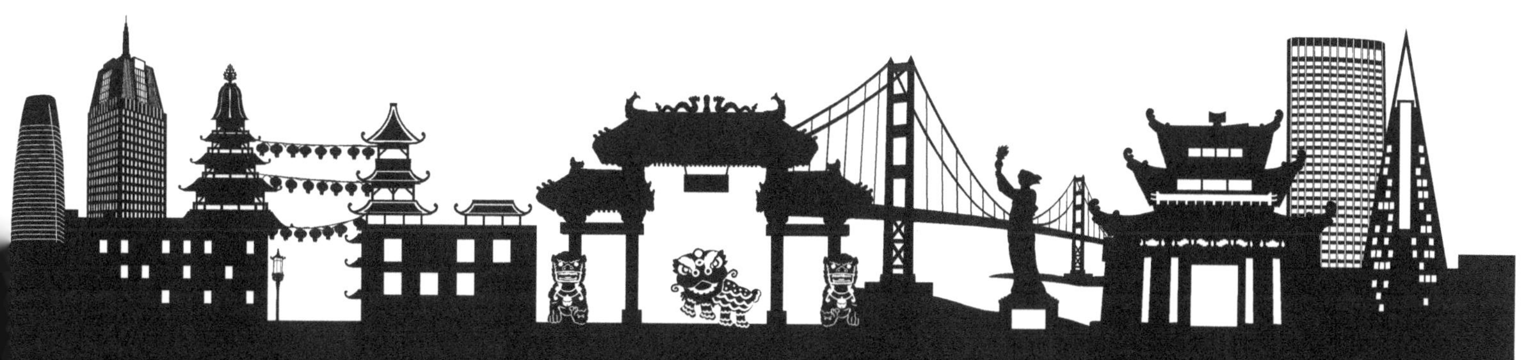

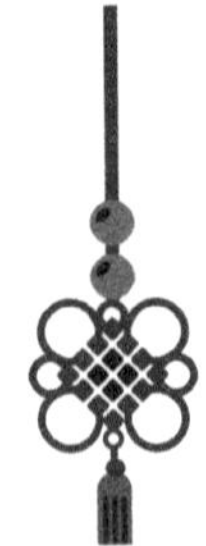

DRAGON GATE
龙门

Enter Chinatown through the pagoda-style Dragon Gate to encounter another world
in the heart of San Francisco. Beyond its portals, you will find a vibrant community
and many treasures, from teas and dim sum, silk, gems, and antiques to modern
knickknacks — it is a world waiting to be discovered.

Dedicated in 1970, this iconic landmark stands at the intersection of Bush Street
and Grant Avenue. Clayton Lee, a Chinese American architect, drew inspiration from
ceremonial entrances to Chinese villages and used the traditional stone, wood, and
green tiles as building materials. It is the only authentic Chinatown Gate
in North America.

The two-tiered structure was built according to the principles of Feng Shui.
This practice involves the careful placement of objects to harmonize individuals
with their surroundings.

Thus, the Dragon Gate's three jade green portals face south. The male lion holds a ball
under his paws, representing unity, while the female has a lion cub under her paw,
a symbol of fertility. The pair offers protection from evil spirits and brings good luck
to the community beyond.

The Chinese characters on each portal represent the core values in Chinese society.
The west portal reads "trust; peace." The east portal reads "respect; love."
The gilded words on the wooden sign of the central portal read "All under heaven
is for the good of the people," a quote from the onetime resident of Chinatown
and "Father of Modern China," Dr. Sun Yat-sen.

Today, the Dragon Gate continues to attract visitors from around the world
and is one of the most popular photo spots in San Francisco. Take a moment
to stand back and absorb its beauty before you enter Chinatown to explore
this unique community!

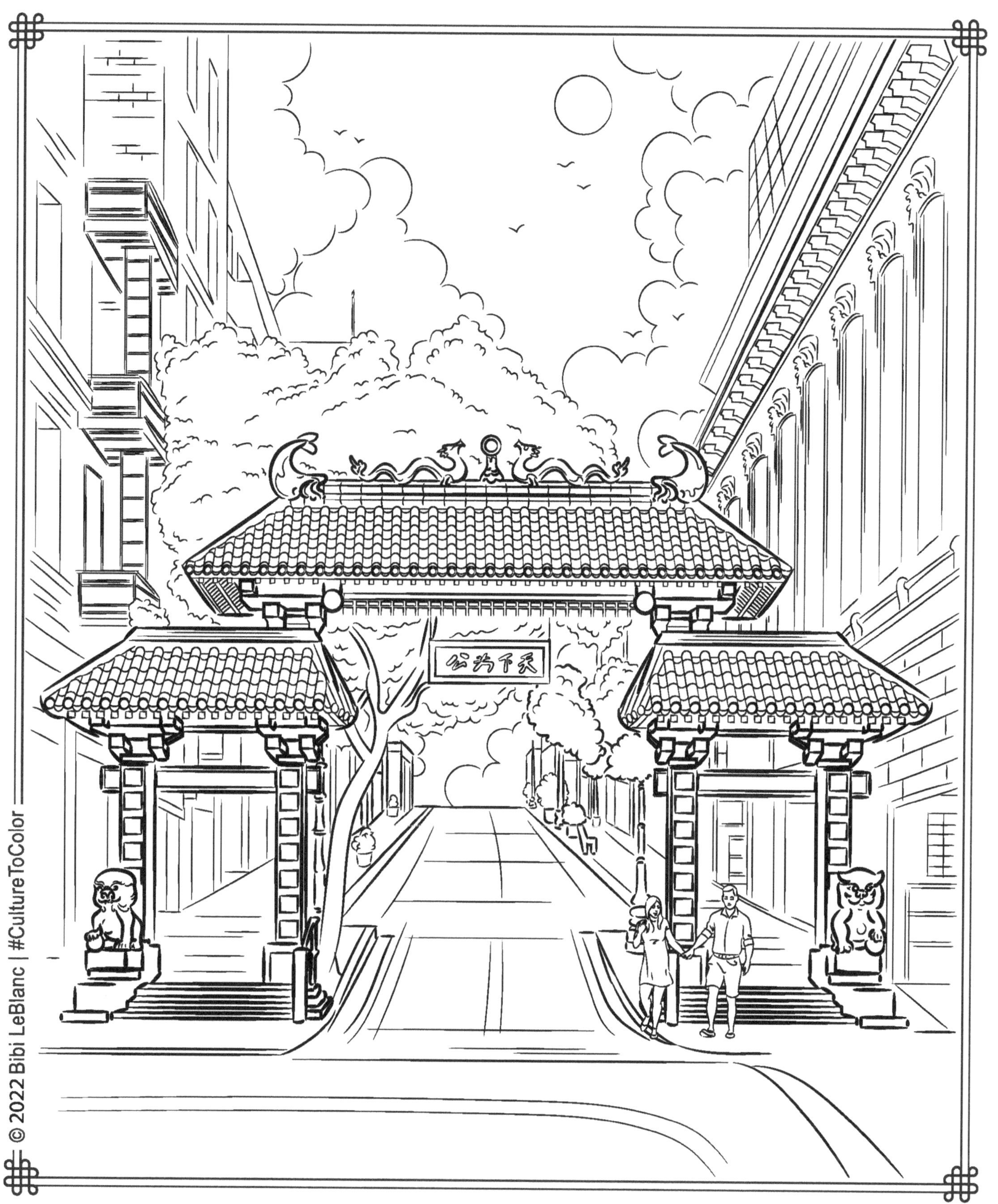

Dragon Gate

龙门

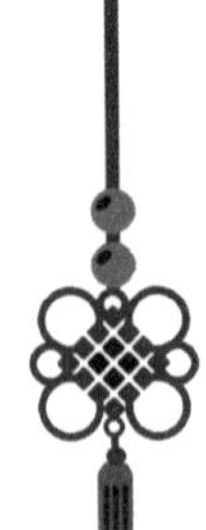

Grant Avenue
都板街

Step through the Dragon Gate and find yourself on Grant Avenue, the heart of Chinatown. This street is known the world over for its wide variety of shops and restaurants, and as the location for many celebrations and festivals.

Grant Avenue was the first street of Yerba Buena, the settlement that would later become San Francisco. Most of the original buildings on Grant Avenue were destroyed in the 1906 earthquake and fires and rebuilt using traditional Chinese design and architectural elements in order to attract visitors.

Stroll down Grant Avenue, and revel in the uniqueness of this location: Dragon streetlamps, Chinese signs, red lanterns strung across the street, and pagoda-style rooftops form the backdrop to the hustle and bustle of this vibrant street.

Have fun exploring the variety of stores full of eclectic treasures, ranging from Buddha statues to antique furniture, parasols, fortune cats, back scratchers, mahjong and other games, kites, silk robes, woks, and San Francisco memorabilia.

Here you will find the perfect gifts to take home for your family and friends!

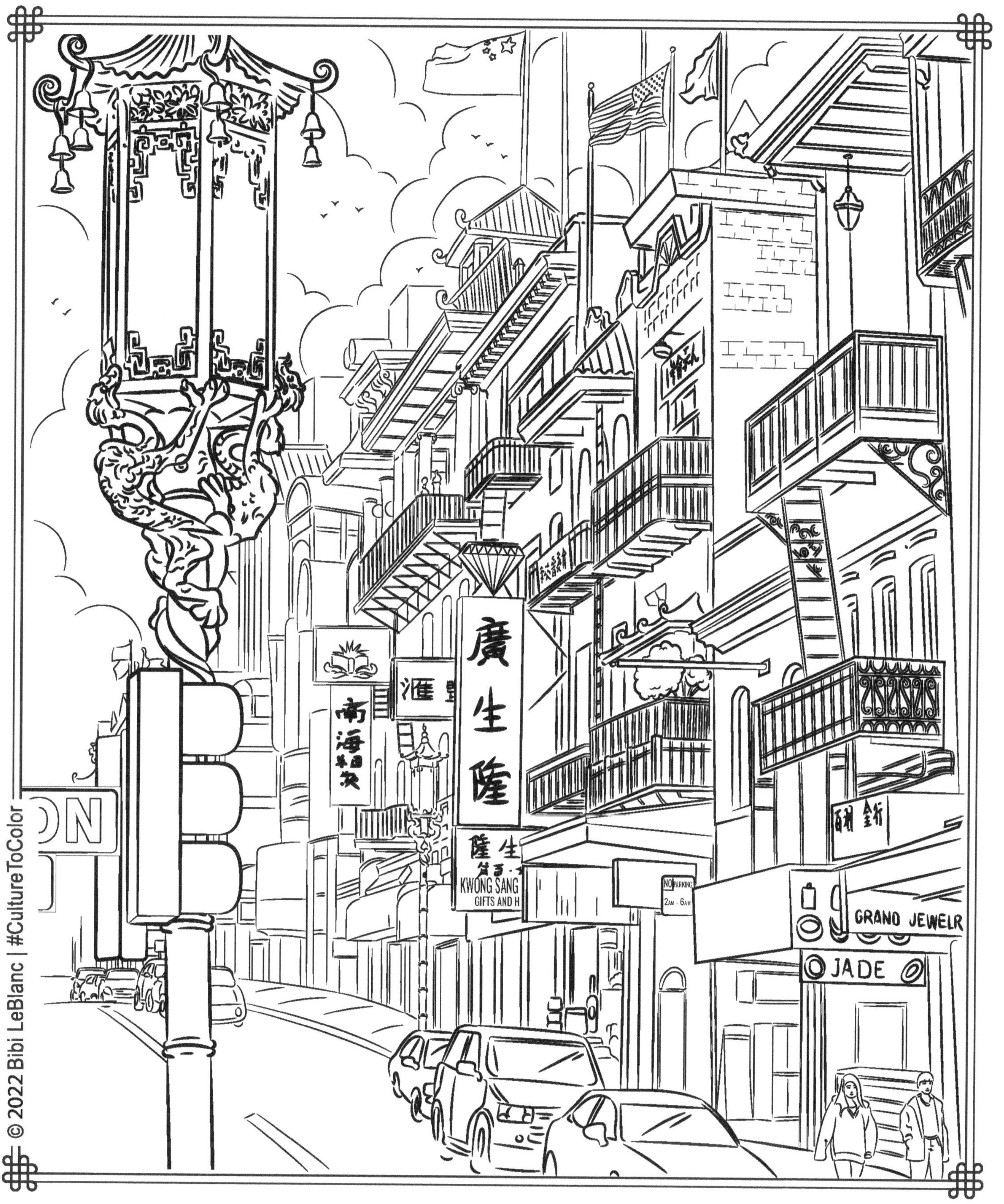

GRANT AVENUE

都板街

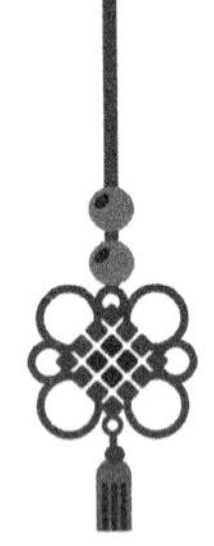

Dragons & Dragon Dance
龙与舞龙

The Chinese dragon is a magnificent and fierce-looking creature. It has become the symbol of China and Chinese culture. Depictions of dragons can be found everywhere — on buildings, in legends, astrology, sculptures, paintings, names, and, of course, festivals.

In contrast to the savage dragons in Western culture, Chinese dragons are benevolent beings and symbols of luck, wisdom, wealth, power, and nobility.

Today, Dragon Dances are an essential part of the Chinese New Year celebrations and other festivals. During a Dragon Dance, the performers raise and lower poles holding up the dragon — sometimes 100 feet long, and made of paper, silk, and bamboo — making it undulate through the streets of Chinatown. The dragon is believed to scare away evil spirits and bad luck.

Did You Know?

The dragon is the only mythical animal in the Chinese zodiac.
People born in the Year of the Dragon are said to be kindhearted, intelligent, successful and courageous, and to possess leadership skills.

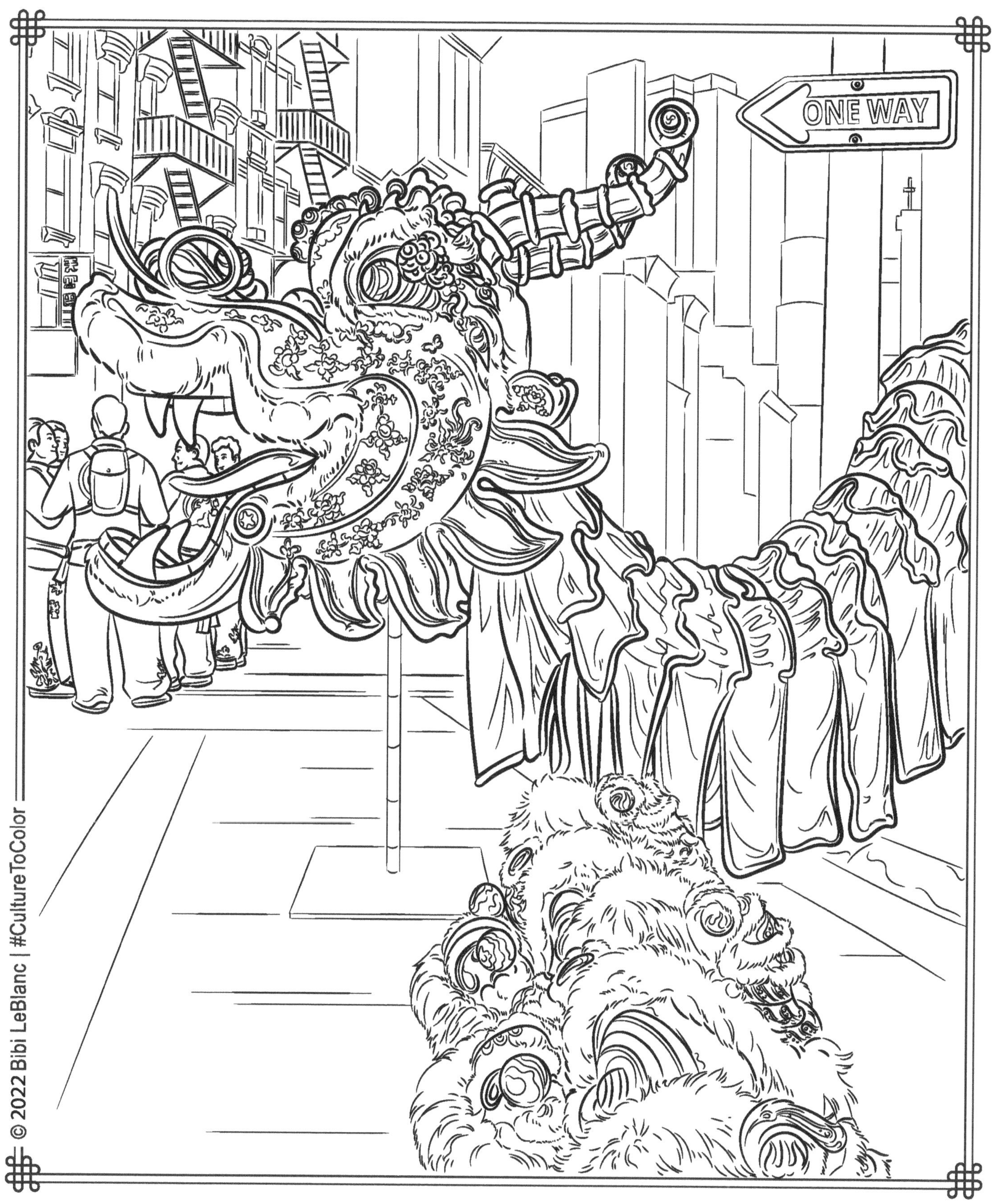

Dragons & Dragon Dance

龙与舞龙

Chinese New Year Symbols
中国新年标记

The Chinese New Year is the most significant among all Chinese festivals and holidays. New Year traditions are an essential part of Chinese culture. You will notice symbols associated with this celebration everywhere. Each of these symbols has its tradition and deep meaning.

On New Year's Eve, family members gather in the home of the most revered person in the family, typically a parent or grandparent. Traditional New Year's activities include cleaning and decorating the house, wearing new clothes, hosting family reunions with large meals, giving good-luck gifts, honoring the zodiac animal, and relaxing on New Year's Day.

Red Envelopes

Red envelopes are among the most common gifts. These come in many sizes, and have designs ranging from simple to sophisticated. Traditionally handed out only by married people to children and the unmarried, the envelopes are full of symbolic meaning and have the power to ward off evil spirits. The inclusion of money is meant to bring health and peace to the recipient.

Citrus Trees

You will find tangerine and orange trees all around town, in homes, offices, and shops during this time. The fruits' bright orange color resembles gold, and is considered an auspicious symbol of wealth, good luck, and abundant happiness.

Firecrackers

Setting off firecrackers is rooted in ancient Chinese customs, and has long been part of New Year's traditions to scare off evil spirits and bad luck. Legend tells of loud firecrackers frightening away the mythical monster Nian.

Food

Dishes with lucky symbolic meanings are served during the 16-day festivities to bring good luck for the coming year. Some of the most common foods are fish (prosperity), dumplings (great wealth), rice cakes (increased income or position), and spring rolls (wealth). Not only are the dishes themselves important, but also significant is the manner in which they are prepared, served, and eaten!

Fun Fact

According to legend, the use of knives or scissors on New Year's Day is considered bad luck — their use may "cut off" your good fortune for the upcoming year.

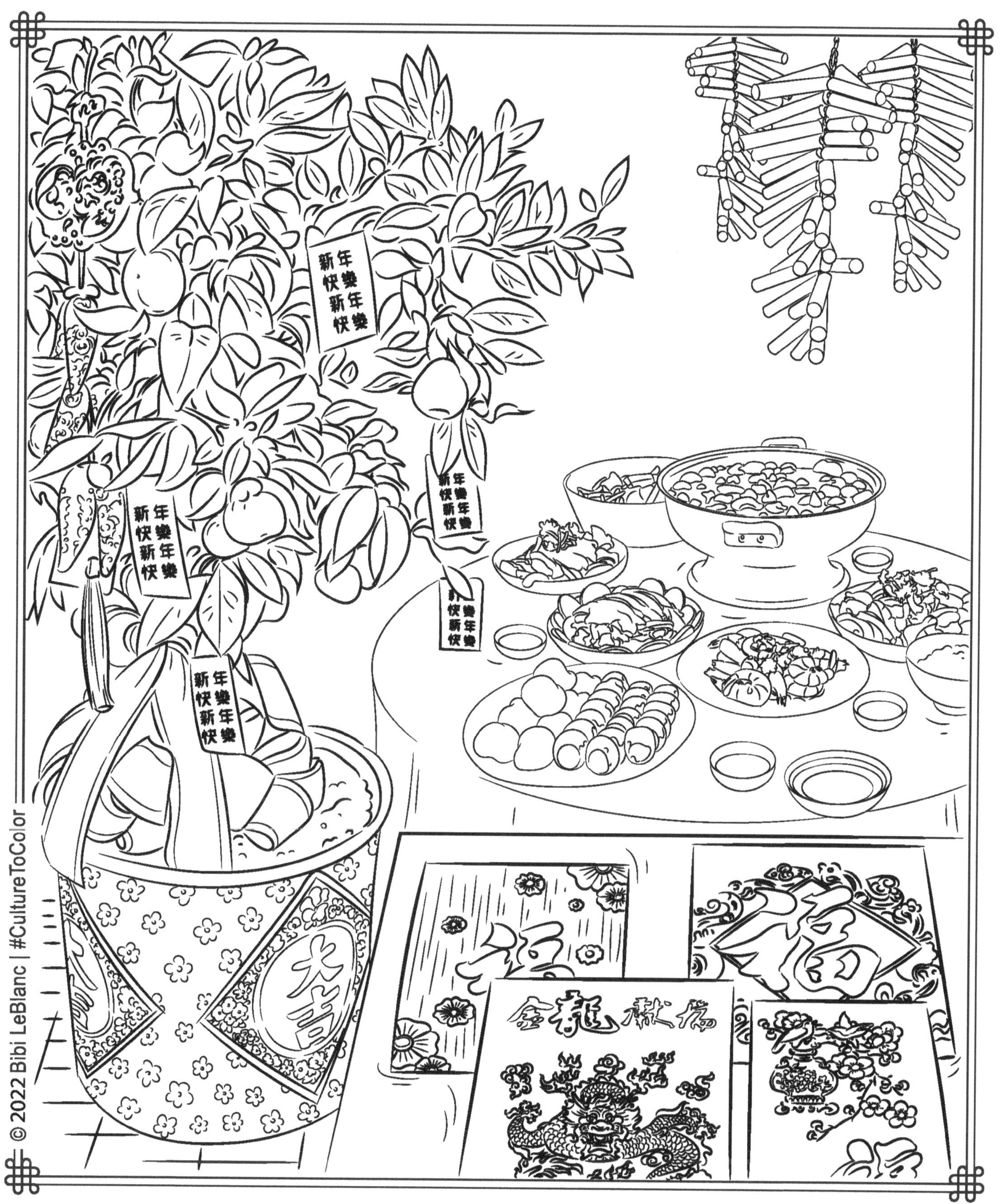

Chinese New Year Symbols

中国新年标记

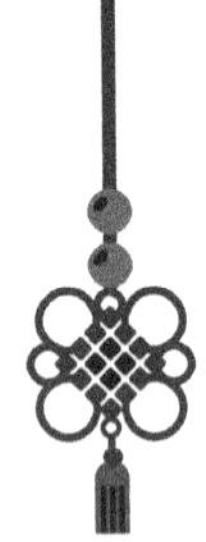

CHINESE NEW YEAR PARADE
中国新年游行

Visit Chinatown early in the year and attend the annual San Francisco
Chinese New Year Festival and Parade. The parade date changes every year,
and typically falls on a day between mid-January and mid-February. Dating back
to the mid-19th century, this spectacular event is the oldest of its kind outside of Asia.

Traditionally, this Chinatown extravaganza consists of drummers, stilt walkers,
elaborate floats, schoolchildren in costumes, lion dancers, marching bands, acrobats,
the ubiquitous dragon, and so much more, bringing to life colorful, entertaining,
and educational elements of Chinese culture and tradition.

It is listed as one of the top 10 parades in the world by the International
Festivals & Events Association. Watched by thousands of in-person spectators
and millions of television viewers around the globe, this parade is the largest
Asian cultural celebration in North America.

This is an event you don't want to miss — it is a dazzling feast for your eyes
and camera!

GUNG HAY FAT CHOY!
恭喜发财!

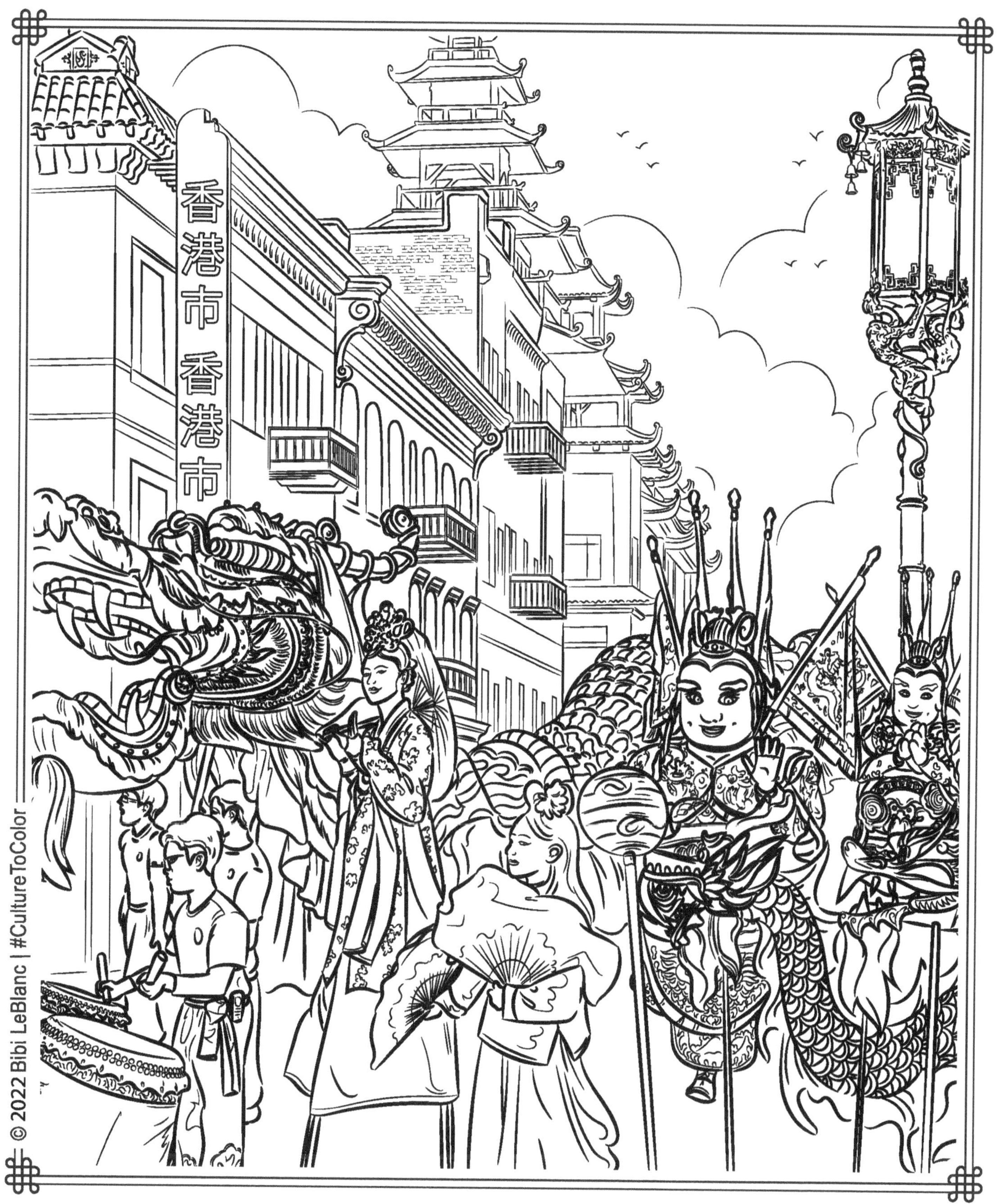

Chinese New Year Parade

中国新年游行

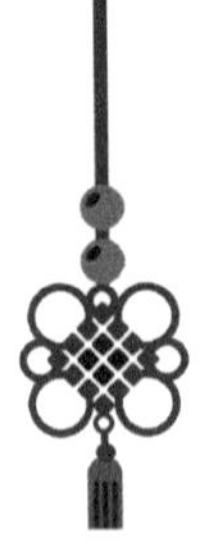

EAST WEST BANK
FORMER CHINESE TELEPHONE EXCHANGE

華美銀行—原中国电话局

743 Washington Street

This eye-catching edifice is one of the oldest Asian-style buildings in Chinatown.
It was erected in 1909 after the 1906 earthquake and fire destroyed the
original structure.

The alluring building was once home to the largest Chinese Telephone Exchange
outside of China. The operators had to memorize thousands of phone numbers
and manually connect calls by plugging wires into switchboards. At its peak,
the exchange serviced more than 3,000 private residences, businesses, and
public phones. The women had to know all the languages spoken in Chinatown,
including the different dialects, and English. Some days they handled more
than 13,000 calls.

The exchange became a major tourist attraction. Visitors would peek through
the windows to watch the operators, wearing embroidered silk dresses, in action.

The exchange closed in 1949, by which time rotary-dial telephones made switchboard
operators obsolete. Today, this stunning structure is a functioning bank, and remains
one of Chinatown's most distinctive and photographed buildings.

DID YOU KNOW?

The Telephone Exchange provided delivery services to the Chinatown community
long before modern-day providers. According to a Chinese Digest article, by 1911,
the exchange had 474 business subscribers and 600 residential subscribers,
allowing members of the community to do their shopping over the phone.

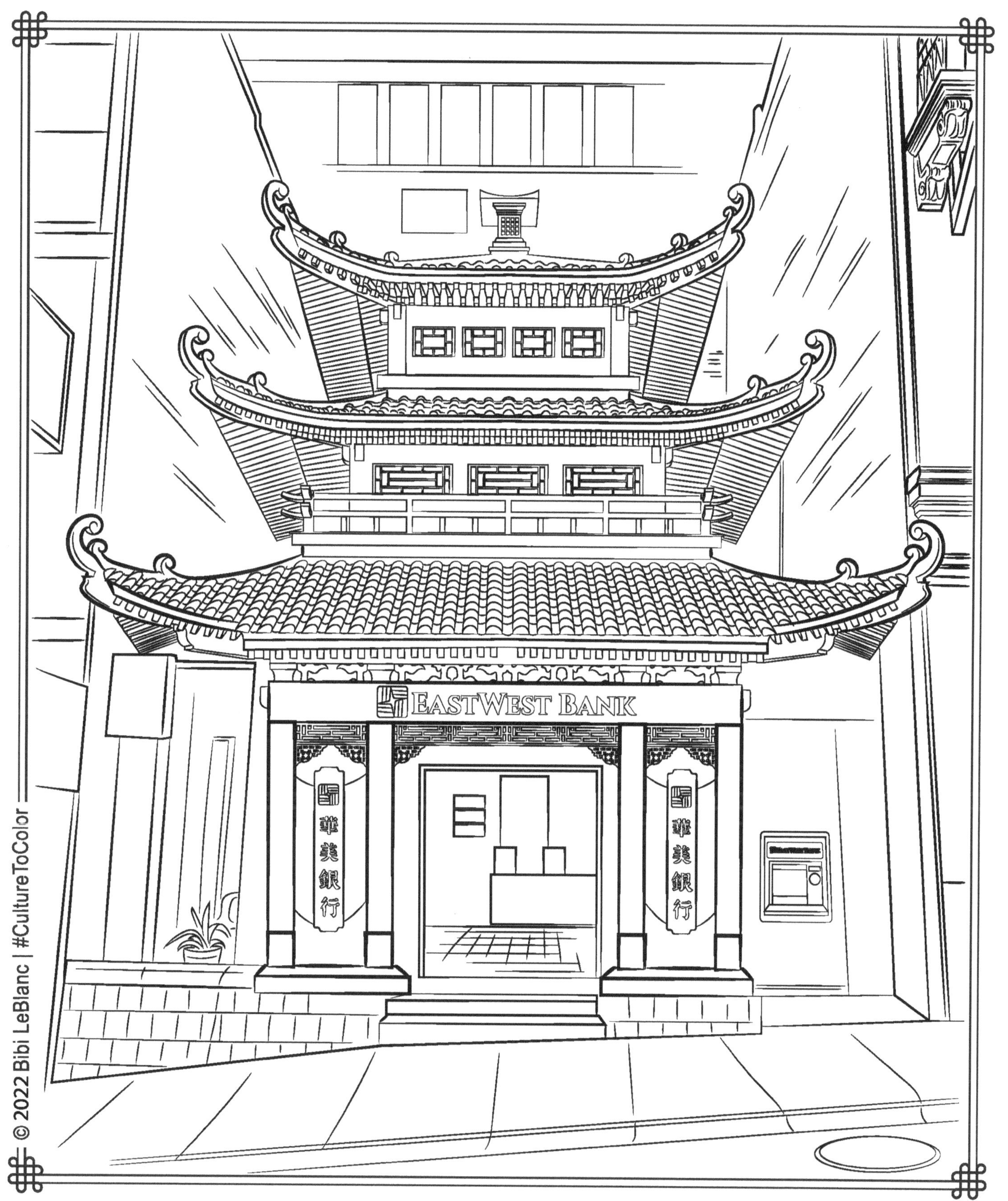

East West Bank
Former Chinese Telephone Exchange

華美銀行—原中国电话局

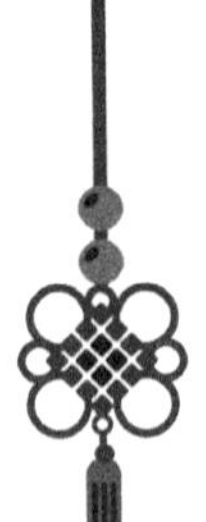

TEA

茶 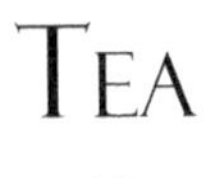

If you would like to retreat from the hustle and bustle of Chinatown and find some peace and quiet, stop in one of the tea shops. Some are modeled after wine bars and offer complimentary tea tastings. Chat with your host and learn about the history of tea, its many varieties, and its health benefits.

Tea, an essential aspect of Chinese culture, is produced from young leaves and leaf buds. Harvested from tea trees, these raw materials go through an elaborate process of fermentation and roasting that results in the final product. The main naturally occurring ingredients in tea are essential oils, caffeine, and tannins.

Today, tea is among the most popular beverages in the world. Visit a Chinatown tea shop to find out why, and choose from a wide variety of loose-leaf teas and tea sets to take home.

DID YOU KNOW?

The tea ceremony remains one of the most significant traditions in modern Chinese weddings. The bride and groom serve tea to parents, in-laws, and other family members, thus showing respect to their elders, who in turn show their acceptance of the union of the two families.

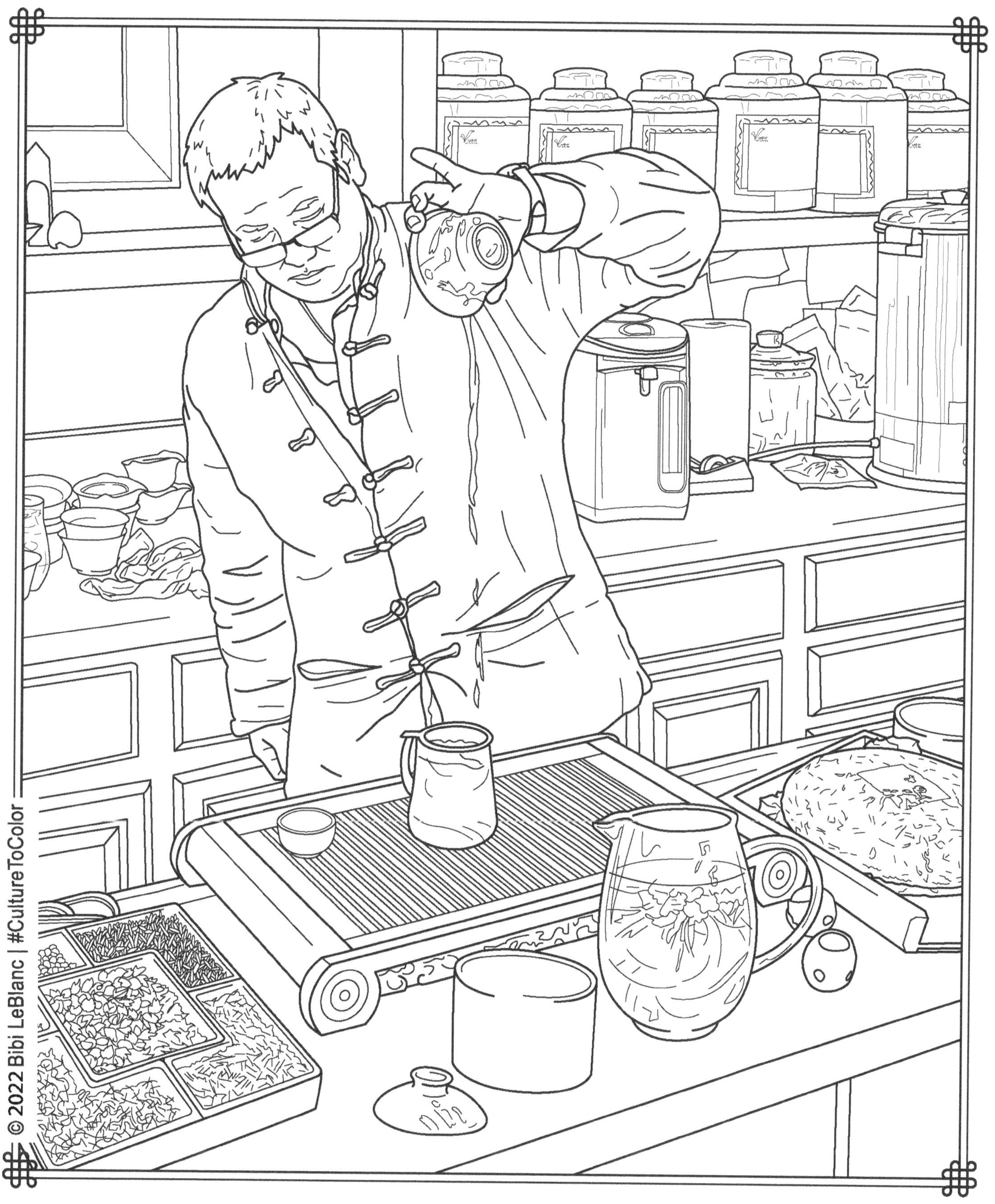

Tea

茶

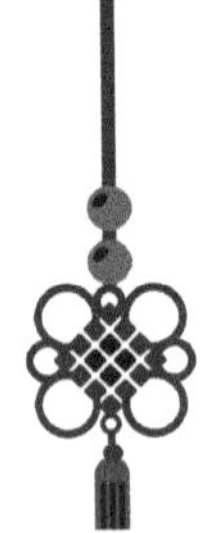

CABLE CARS

缆车

Hop on a cable car for a unique ride to Chinatown. An iconic mode
of transportation, San Francisco cable cars run along two sides of Chinatown.

Andrew Smith Hallidie invented cable cars about 150 years ago after observing
an accident involving horses struggling to pull carts up the steep hills
on wet cobblestones.

Today, San Francisco's cable cars are loved and recognized around the world.
They have changed little and have climbed the city's hills at a steady 9 mph
since 1873. A century-and-a-half later, 40 cable cars are still in operation and serve
millions of people a year. It is the world's last manually operated cable car system.
Go for a leisurely ride and enjoy unforgettable views of San Francisco and Chinatown.

The nearby Cable Car Museum showcases the history of the San Francisco cable car
system. There you can see the cables that pull the cars up and down the streets
of San Francisco. It's a fun and interesting stop.

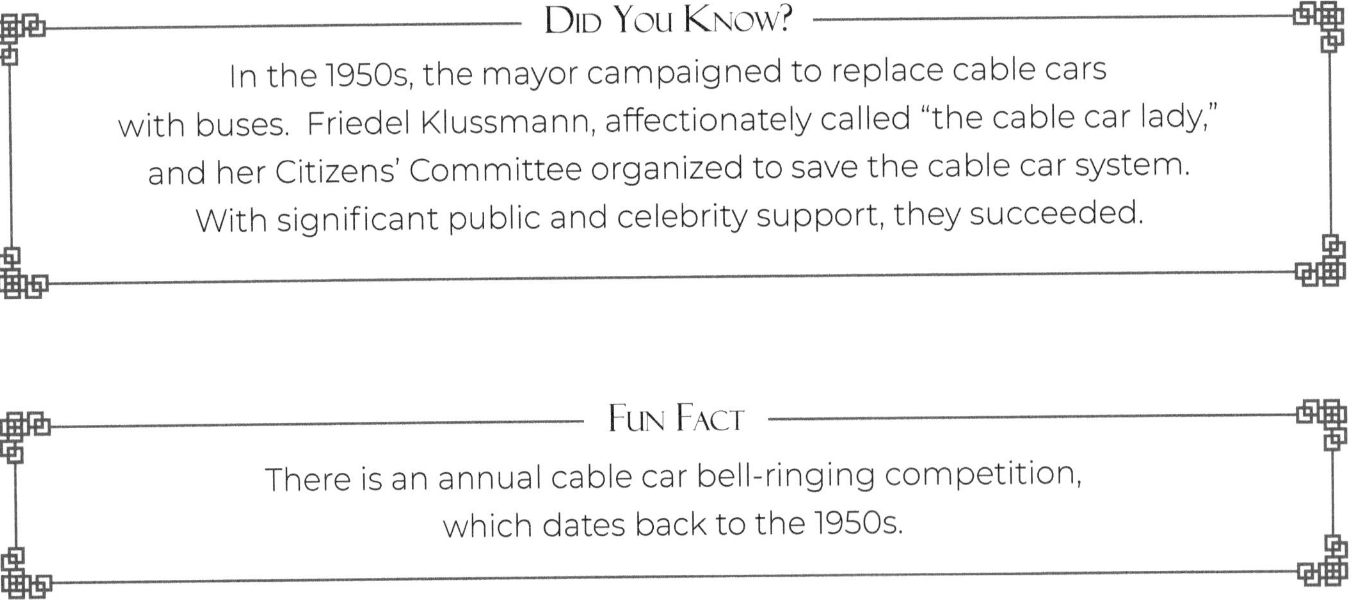

DID YOU KNOW?

In the 1950s, the mayor campaigned to replace cable cars
with buses. Friedel Klussmann, affectionately called "the cable car lady,"
and her Citizens' Committee organized to save the cable car system.
With significant public and celebrity support, they succeeded.

FUN FACT

There is an annual cable car bell-ringing competition,
which dates back to the 1950s.

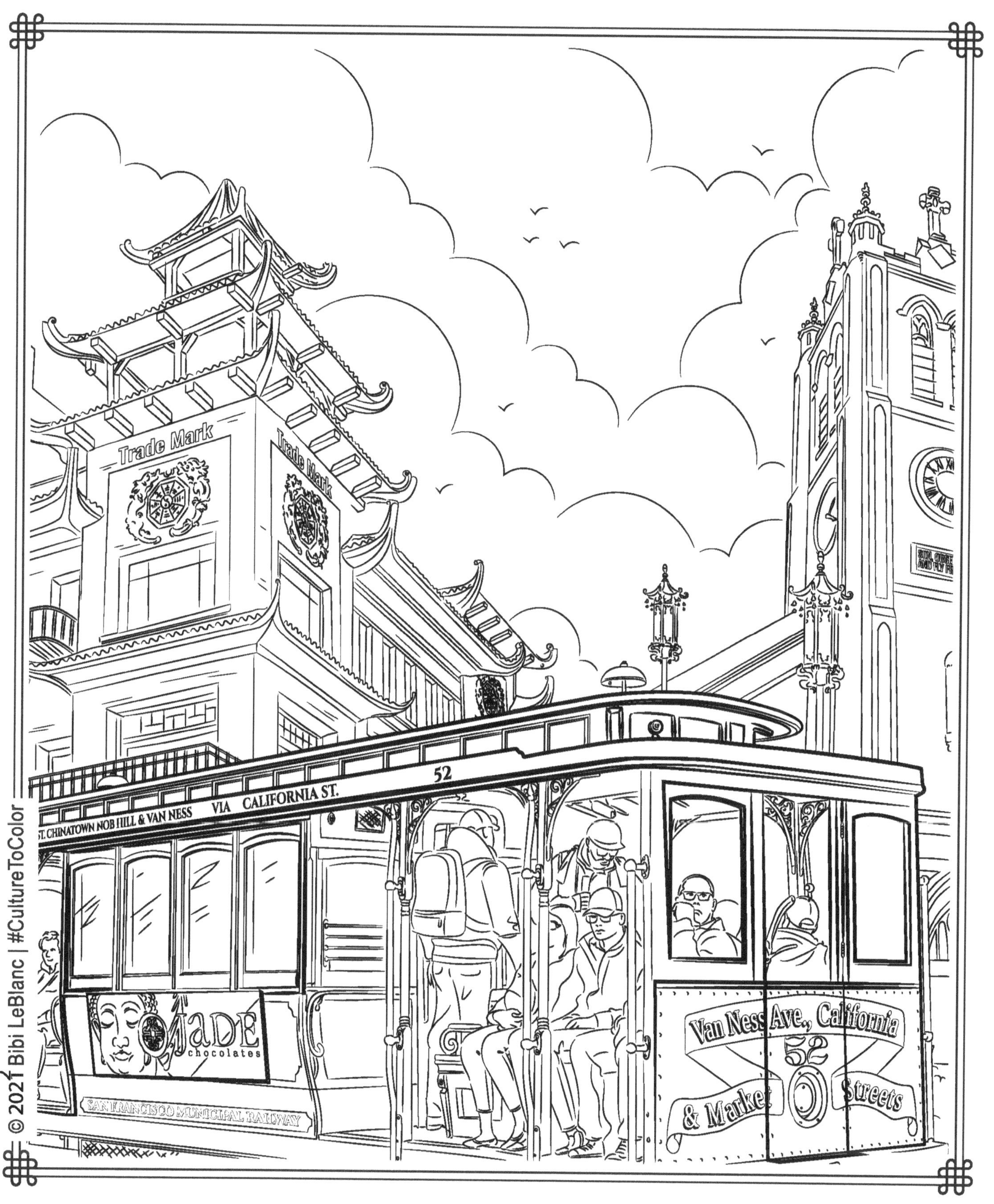

CABLE CARS

缆车

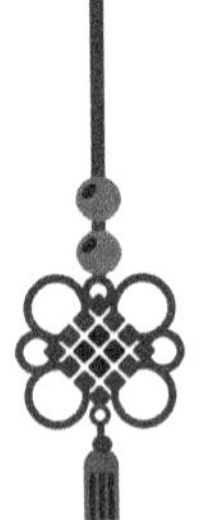

MAHJONG
麻将

As you stroll through Chinatown, chances are you will hear the shuffling
of mahjong tiles, sometimes referred to as "the twittering of sparrows,"
coming from behind many doors. Mahjong is a prominent part of local culture.
Mahjong loosely translates to "sparrow," but most San Franciscans refer to it as MJ.

The game originated in China. Many believe its roots go back to the time of Confucius,
but the oldest historical record dates back only to the 1880s.

One of the most popular games in Chinatown, mahjong is a complex, fast-paced
tile game of skill and strategy. It is played by men and women, wealthy and poor
alike. Four participants play with a set of tiles and dice, often for hours, taking turns
drawing, organizing, and discarding tiles. To win a game, players use both offensive and
defensive strategies. The goal is to complete the best hand as quickly as possible
while not discarding tiles advantageous to the other players. To get a mahjong,
players must arrange their tiles into four sets and a pair.

Mahjong is a way to socialize and a source of entertainment at gatherings
and celebrations. It is often played during New Year's festivities.

You can find mahjong games, from plain to fancy, in many of the Chinatown stores.

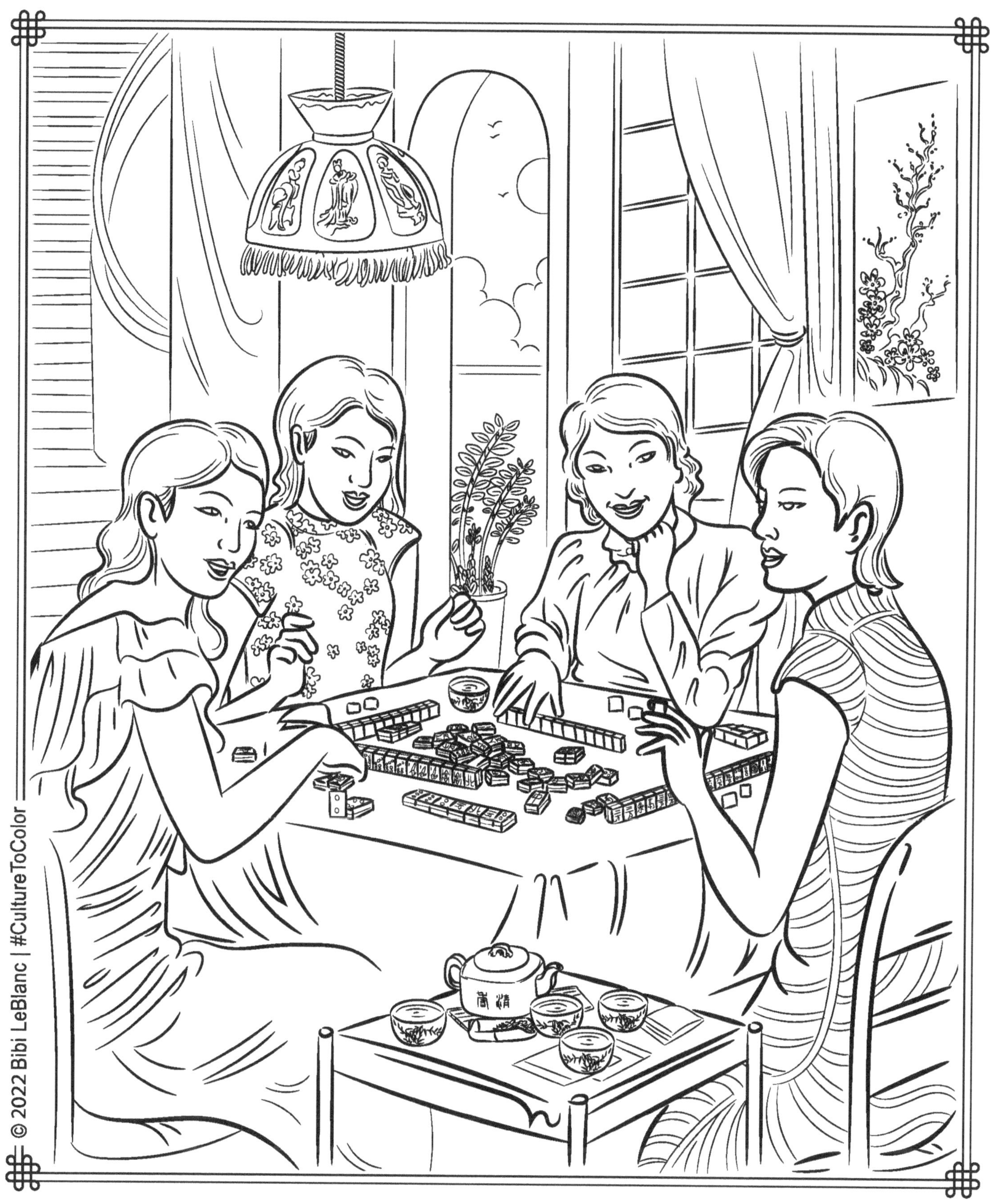

Mahjong

麻将

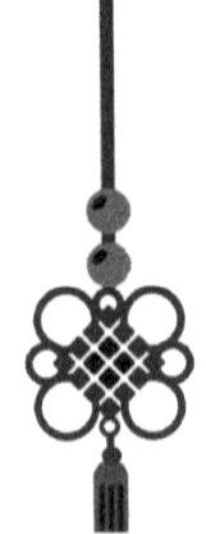

CHINATOWN RESTAURANTS
唐人街的餐厅

One of the best aspects of Chinatown is the eclectic variety of restaurants.
From street food to Michelin-rated restaurants, the array of delectable dishes available
will delight your taste buds!

Authentic Chinese cooking uses fresh ingredients and is considered one of the most
healthful cuisines in the world. A combination of the five essential flavors — salty, sour,
bitter, spicy, and sweet — must be balanced to create a satisfying meal.

Chinatown has many restaurants from which to choose, ranging from small
takeout hideaways to upscale, elegant restaurants with dazzling décor. You might even
find yourself in a dining room you've seen on one of the travel and food shows.

Try takeout from one of the many dim sum restaurants. Or dine in and select dishes
from a pushcart while enjoying the ambiance of a traditional Chinese restaurant.

For a sweet treat, you can pick up delicious Chinese pastries such as sesame balls,
egg custard tarts or mooncakes at one of the local bakeries!

FUN FACT

A local legend places the origins of chop suey here in Gold Rush-era
San Francisco: When hungry miners arrived at a local restaurant about to close,
the chef scraped leftovers from other plates, added sauce, and served it.
Thus, chop suey was born.

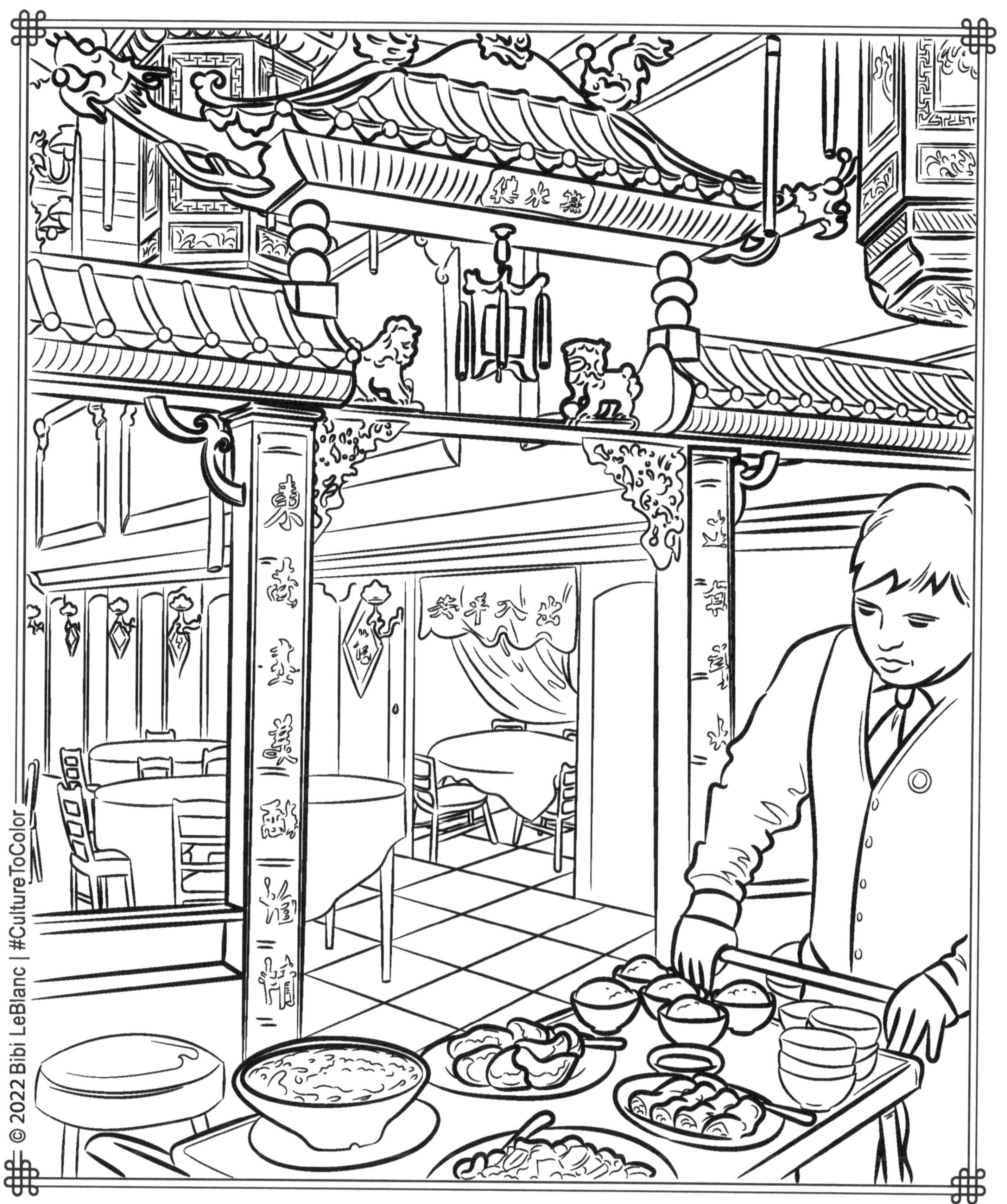

Chinatown Restaurants

唐人街的餐厅

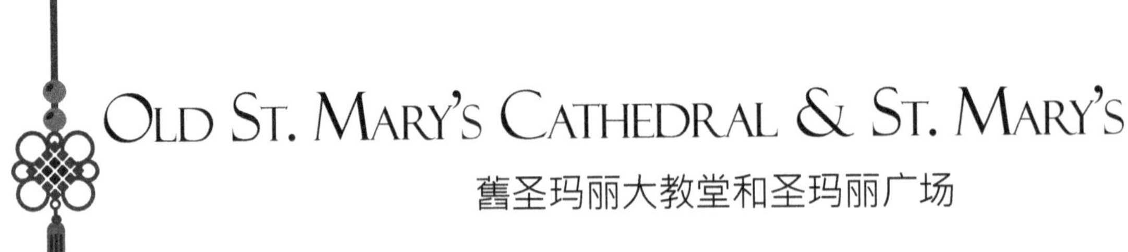

OLD ST. MARY'S CATHEDRAL & ST. MARY'S SQUARE

舊圣玛丽大教堂和圣玛丽广场

660 California Street

Amid a backdrop of traditional Chinese architecture stands a historic
Gothic cathedral, Old St. Mary's, San Francisco's first Catholic church.
When the original cathedral opened in 1854, it was the tallest building in
San Francisco. In 1891, it was replaced by a larger cathedral, which was almost
destroyed during fires that followed the 1906 earthquake. The church was rebuilt
and continued its ministry to the Chinese population. It remains one of the
most prominent buildings in Chinatown. Inside this active parish church,
you can view photos and read texts that relate its fascinating history.

Nearby, St. Mary's Square serves as a neighborhood gathering place where
locals practice tai chi and families use the playground. Others come to view
the Women's Column of Strength and the memorial plaque commemorating
Chinese Americans who served during World War I and World War II.
Additionally, people pay tribute to Dr. Sun Yat-sen, founder of the Republic of China,
memorialized with a 14-foot statue. He liked to read here during his exile years
in San Francisco.

The *Dragon Street Lamps* were originally designed for the Diamond Jubilee Festival
in 1925. Each lamp is painted in the traditional green, red, and gold colors,
and the dragons wrapped around the lamppost symbolize good luck,
fortune, and longevity.

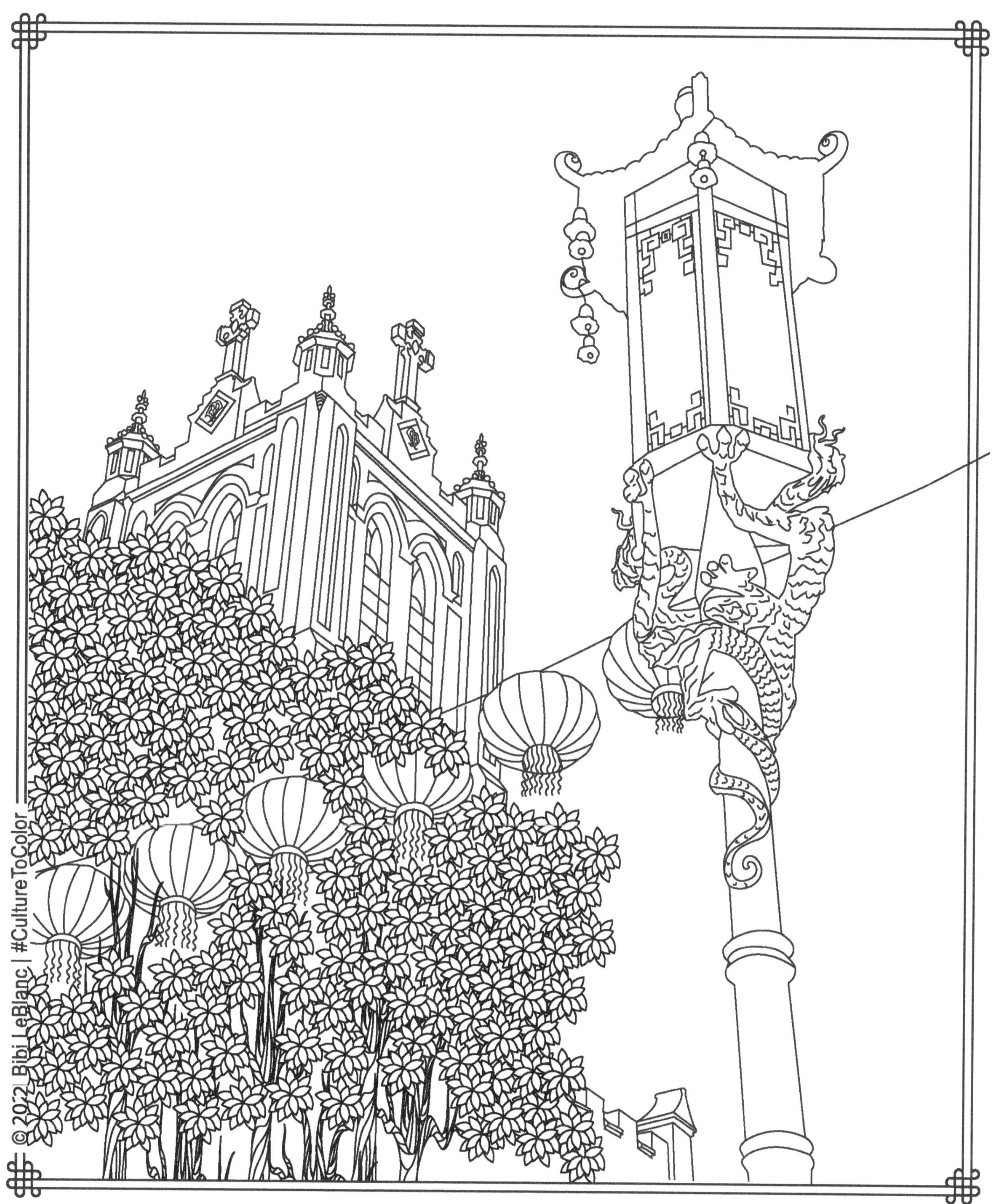

OLD ST. MARY'S CATHEDRAL & ST. MARY'S SQUARE

舊圣玛丽大教堂和圣玛丽广场

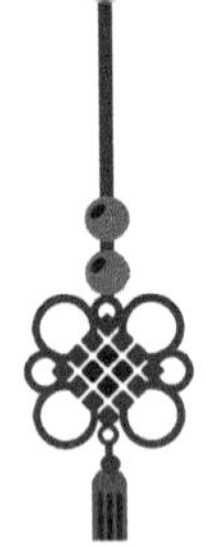

LION DANCE
舞狮

The lion dance is a popular example of Chinese folk culture with a history that goes back thousands of years. It is a traditional dance performed during New Year celebrations, cultural and religious festivals, and other important occasions such as weddings, business openings, or honoring special guests. In Chinese culture, the lion represents strength, wisdom, and longevity. A lion dance is believed to bring prosperity, good luck, and peace.

Performed by two dancers in a colorful lion costume, the lion dance requires strength, agility, and practice. Drums, gongs, and cymbals accompany the dancers as they visit stores, restaurants, and other businesses. The dance typically finishes with a message of good luck from the lion's mouth and firecrackers to scare away evil spirits!

When exploring Chinatown, you might encounter dancing lions in the streets, spreading goodwill and luck to everyone they meet.

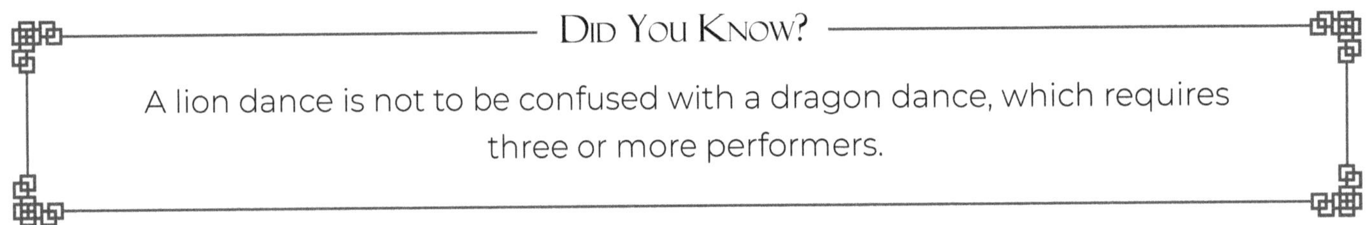

DID YOU KNOW?

A lion dance is not to be confused with a dragon dance, which requires three or more performers.

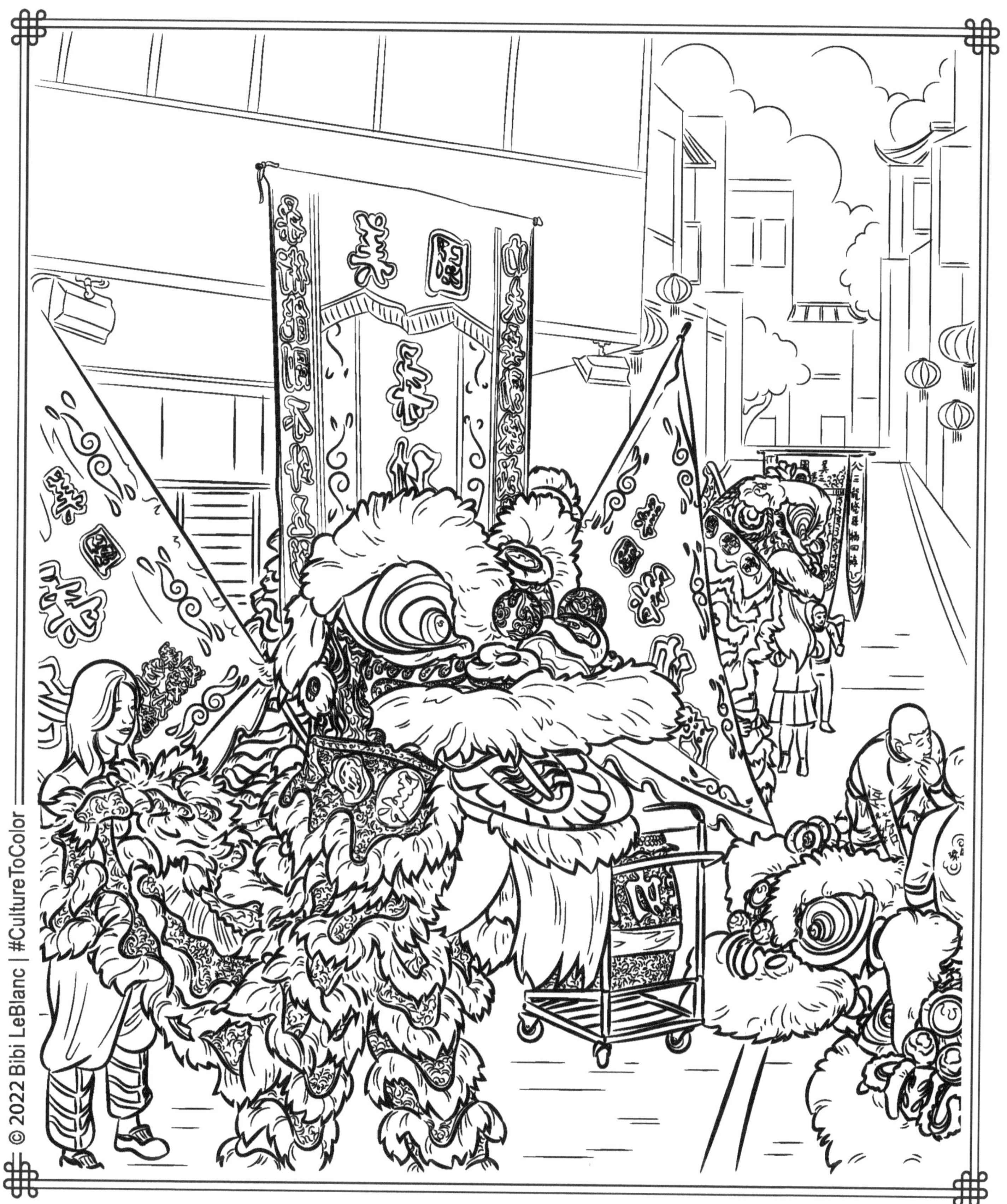

LION DANCE

舞狮

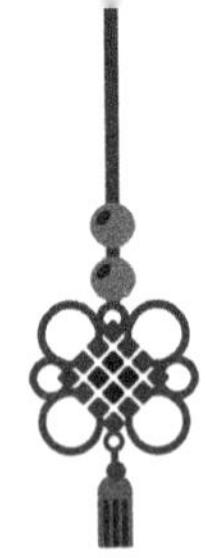

AUTUMN MOON FESTIVAL
中秋节

Visit Chinatown during the annual Autumn Moon Festival — a harvest celebration that dates back more than 3,000 years — and be on the lookout for the Moon Goddess and Moon God.

Dressed in elaborate, historic silk costumes, they recount the legend of Chang'e, who stole the elixir of immortality from her husband, the archer Hou Yi, and became the Goddess of the Moon. Even though Hou Yi was upset, he would leave fresh fruit and other offerings during the Autumn festival, expressing his forgiveness and undying love for his wife.

Each year during the Moon Festival, the streets of Chinatown come alive, attracting tens of thousands of spectators from all corners of the world. The colorful activities begin with a parade along Grant Avenue and continue for two days. Festivities include cultural exhibits, arts and crafts booths, street performances of lion dances, martial arts, acrobats, Chinese opera, ribbon dancers, traditional instrumental music, taiko drummers, puppets, a fashion show, and a youth talent contest. Festivities end with the White Crane Dragon Parade on Sunday afternoon.

Be sure to sample the traditional mooncake, a delicious flaky pastry filled with bean or lotus-seed paste in the shape of the full moon.

The Autumn Moon Festival is a truly unique opportunity to experience cultural diversity at its best! … and maybe even take a photo with the Goddess herself!

DID YOU KNOW?

This ancient harvest festival is celebrated throughout Asian cultures, and was brought to San Francisco by the Chinatown Merchants Association to reinvigorate the community after the 1989 earthquake.

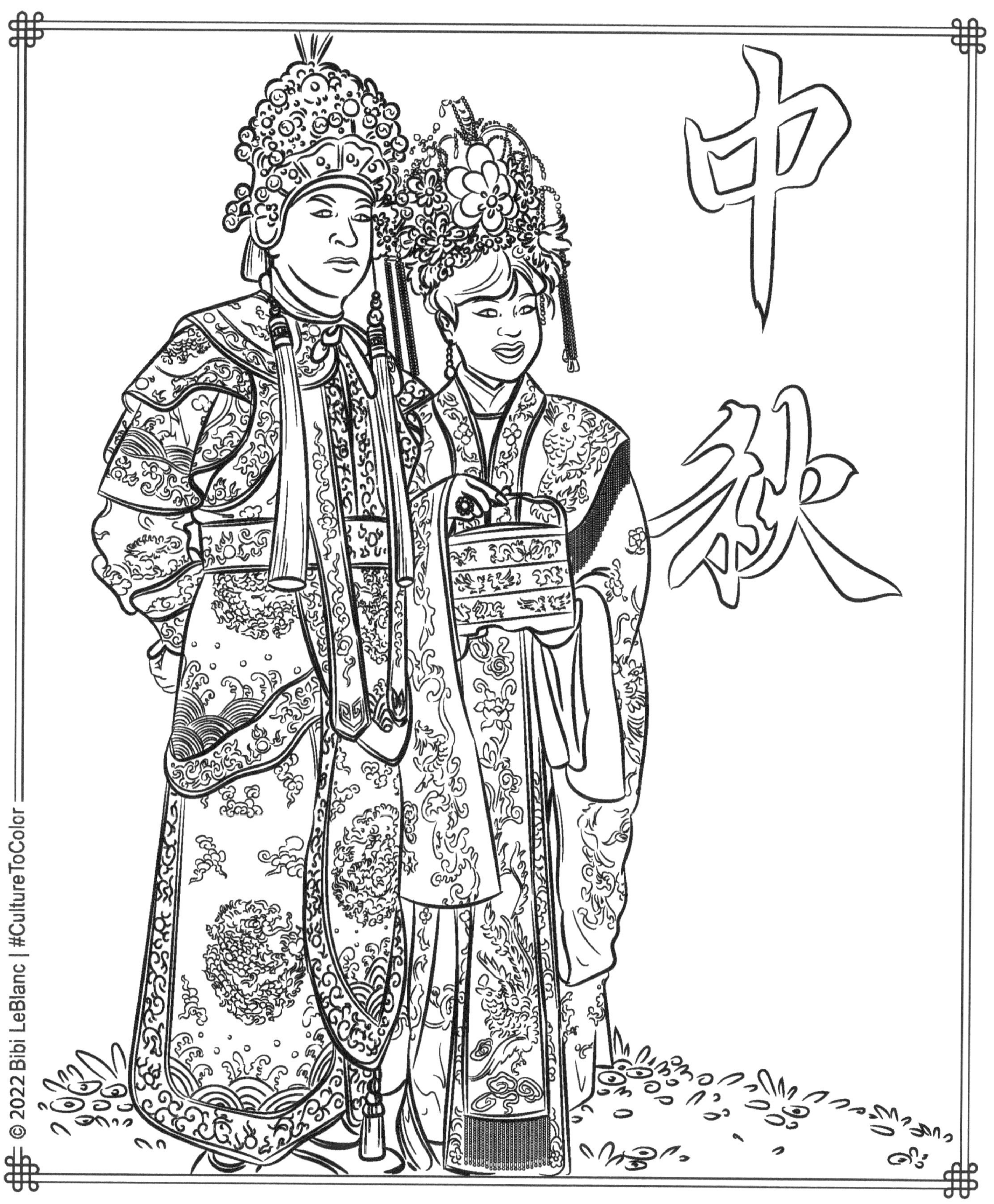

Autumn Moon Festival

中秋节

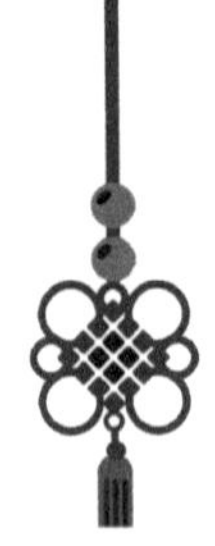

Nam Kue Chinese School

旧金山南侨学校

755 Sacramento Street

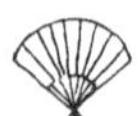

With its traditional architecture and bold colors, this beautiful building
will capture your attention as you explore Chinatown. Nam Kue is a private Chinese
school that offers classes focusing on Chinese language, history, and culture.

Nam Kue means "Nanhai's American-Chinese descendants' school" in Cantonese.
In the late 1910s, Chinese immigrants who had settled in San Francisco established
a school that began with just one classroom, one teacher, and 20 students.
Due to increasing demand, it quickly outgrew its space. The growing need for
more and larger classrooms resulted in the construction of this building,
which was completed in 1926.

Currently, the school offers supplementary instruction focused on Chinese traditions
and culture, such as language, calligraphy, abacus, martial arts, musical instruments,
and traditional dance. It also provides contemporary programs in robotics
and computer sciences. During the summer, it offers enrichment through
its camp program.

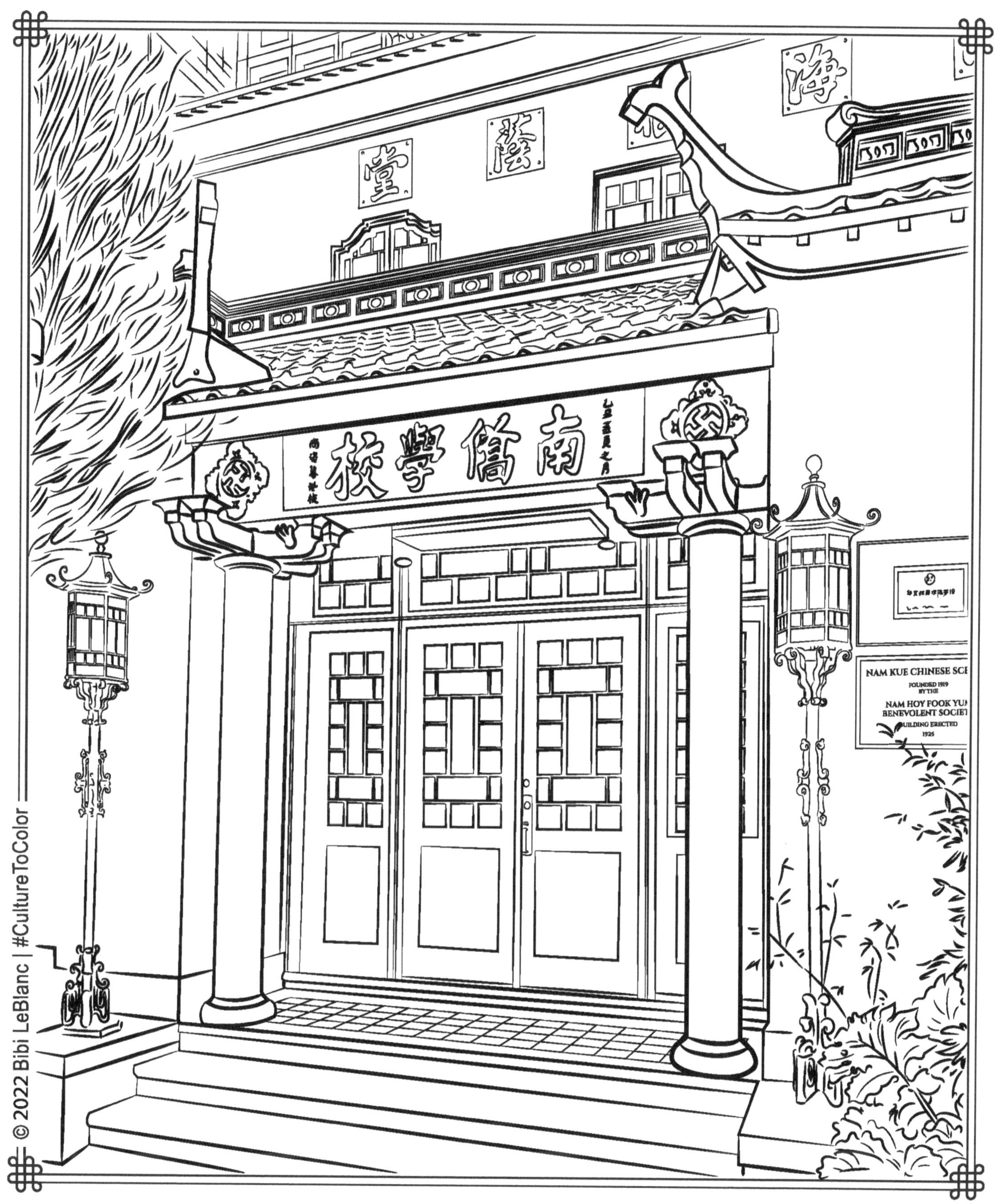

NAM KUE CHINESE SCHOOL

旧金山南侨学校

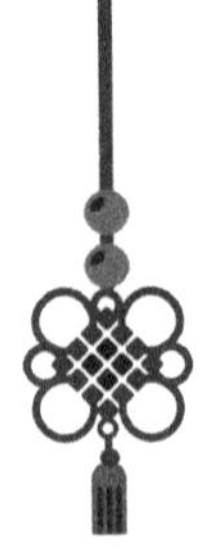

GOLDEN GATE FORTUNE COOKIE FACTORY
金门幸运签语饼公司

56 Ross Alley

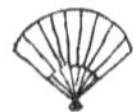

Have you ever wondered where fortune cookies come from or how they are made? Here is your chance to find out. Follow the scent of sweetness to Ross Alley, and pop into the Golden Gate Fortune Cookie Factory. This family-owned bakery has been hand-making fortune cookies since 1962, and is one of San Francisco's hidden treasures.

Feast your eyes on the largest selection of fortune cookies you've ever seen. You can also observe how they are made. The baker blends flour, butter, vanilla, and sugar, to create the batter. Large machines then drip the cookie batter onto round hot plates on a rotating griddle wheel, baking the cookies. The baker pulls them off, gently twists the cookies into their famous shape, and inserts the "fortune."

In addition to the traditional vanilla-flavored cookies, they come in many flavors, sizes, and shapes: plain and sprinkled, chocolate- or strawberry-glazed, regular to giant sizes, and even flat (unfolded) ones. If you'd like to add your own special touch, you can create personalized messages to place inside the cookies.

Visitors from all over the world step off the beaten path to visit this family-friendly little shop where they can sample a warm fresh-off-the-griddle fortune cookie!

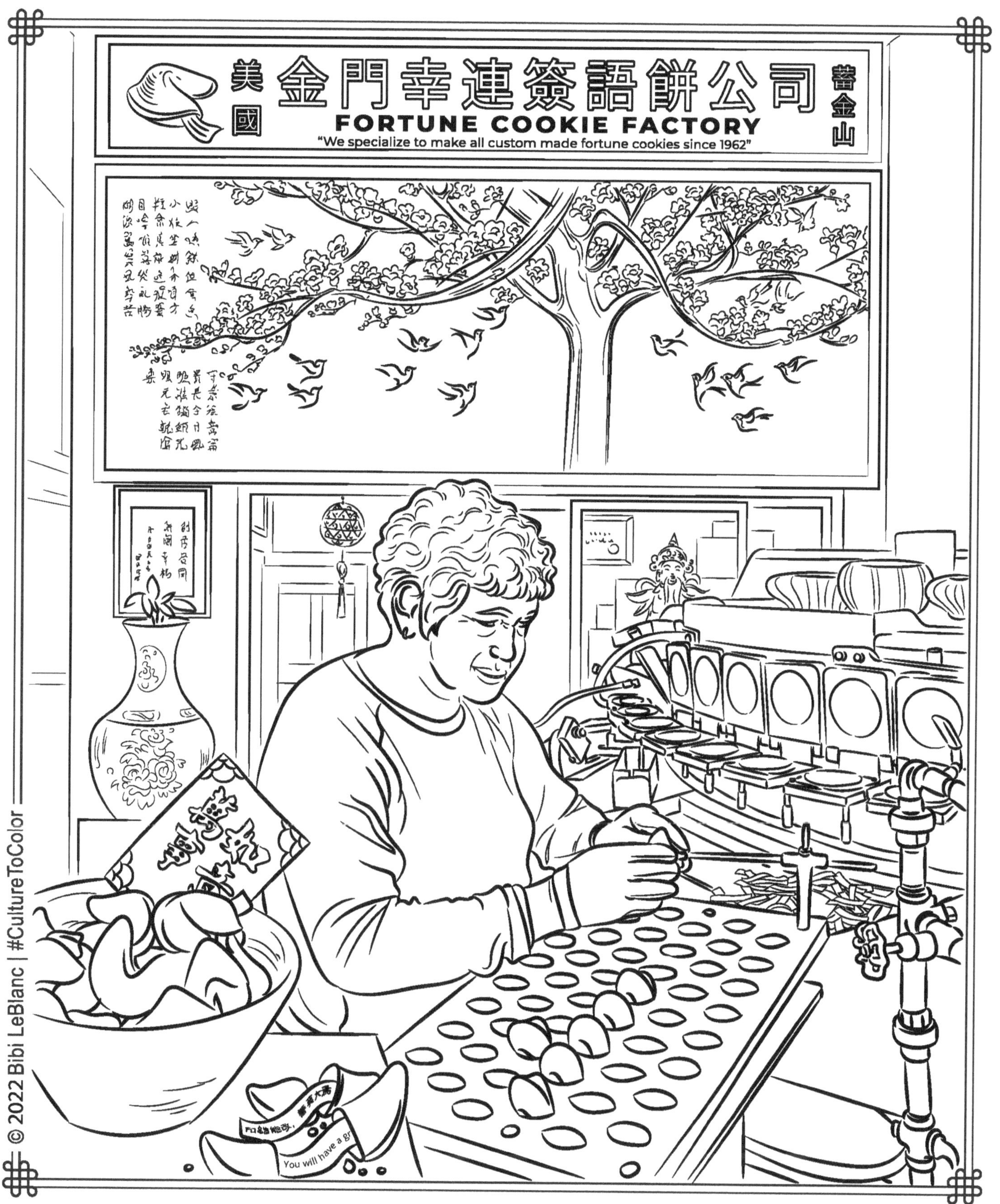

Fortune Cookie Factory

金门幸运签语饼公司

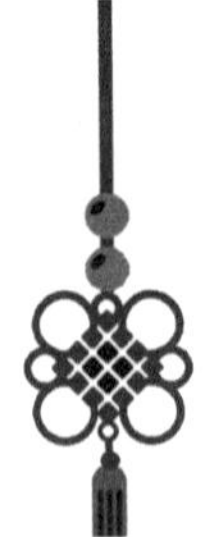

CHINATOWN ARCHITECTURE
中国城建筑

San Francisco Chinatown is known around the world for its striking architecture. Picturesque and colorful, the elaborate designs combined with the ubiquitous red lanterns will make you feel you've entered a different world.

Before 1906, the buildings in Chinatown looked no different from the other buildings in San Francisco. After the devastation wrought by the earthquake and fire, local businessmen seized the opportunity to improve the image of Chinatown. They hired American architects to redesign buildings with a distinctly Chinese look to attract visitors. The result was American-style buildings with colorful pagodas, curled eaves, dragon motifs, and other architectural elements creating the allure that charms visitors to this day.

Estimated to have been invented around A.D. 25-220, Chinese lanterns were originally developed as a light source and for worshipping Buddha. Later, they were also widely used during festivals. The red lanterns swaying in the breeze across Grant Avenue are symbols of good luck and prosperity.

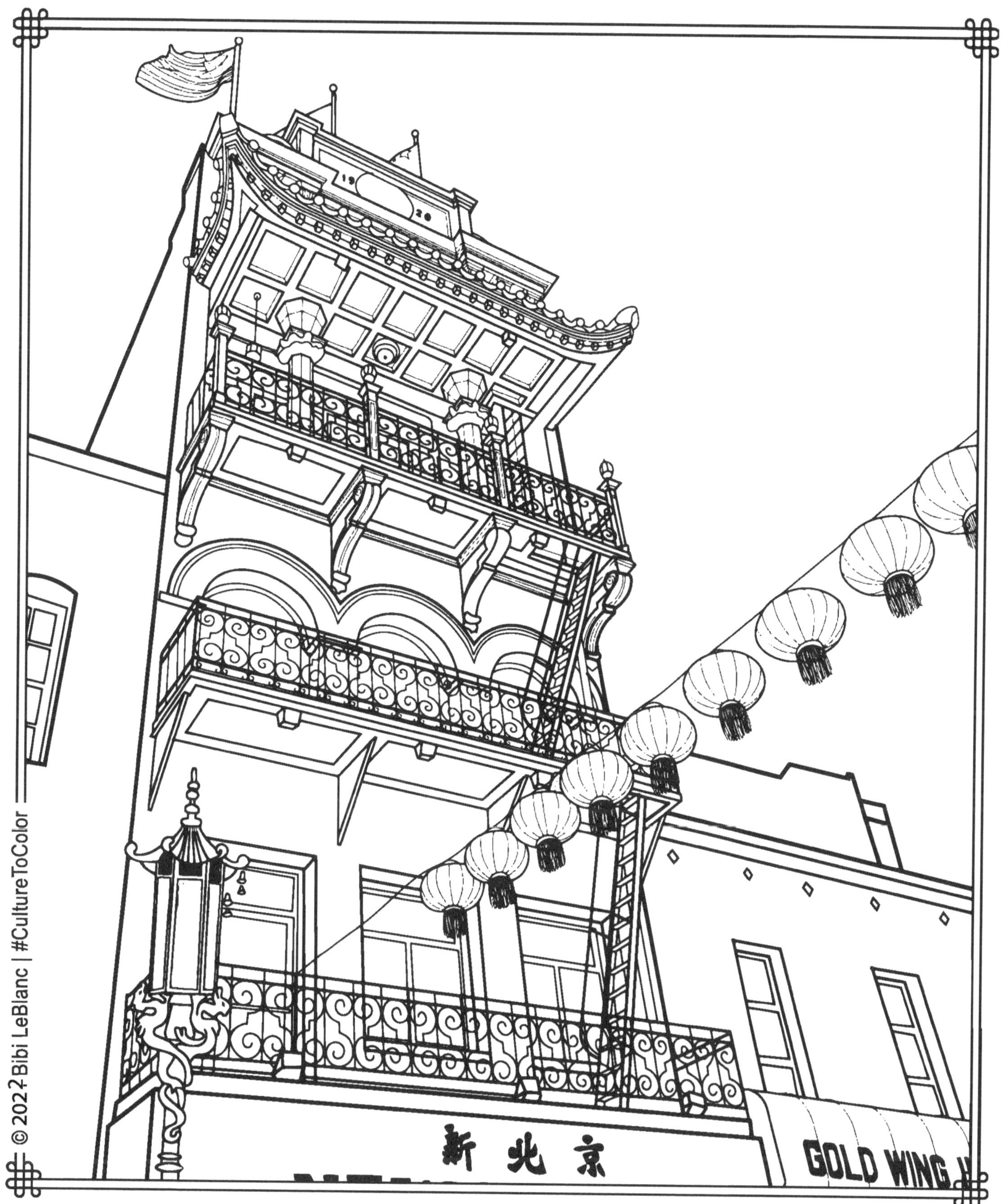

CHINATOWN ARCHITECTURE

中国城建筑

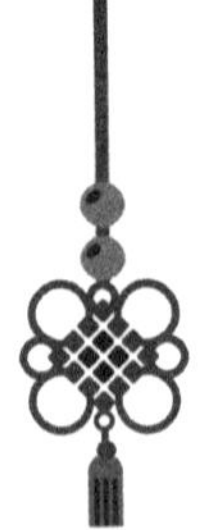

GRANT AVENUE FOLLIES

都板街鬧劇團

The Grant Avenue Follies, a dance group composed of seniors, brings to life the legacy of San Francisco Chinatown's golden nightclub era. The Follies was founded by four professional dancers from San Francisco Chinatown's nightclub culture of the 1950s and '60s. Following doctors' orders to exercise to improve their health, they rediscovered the sheer joy and freedom of dance and reconnected with their youth! Dance classes led to recitals and eventually requests to entertain seniors at various San Francisco Bay Area retirement facilities.

The Follies enjoys a loyal following of seniors, many of whom frequented the Chinatown nightclubs of the 1950s and '60s, such as the Forbidden City, Sky Room, and Shanghai Low — popular and famous clubs at that time. Younger generations interested in their unique roots in Chinatown history also appreciate the Follies and its performances.

Today, the Grant Avenue Follies performs on national and international stages and has been featured in many media stories.

Tip

Visit the Showgirl Magic Museum at the Clarion Performing Arts Center, which pays tribute to the pioneering artists of the time.

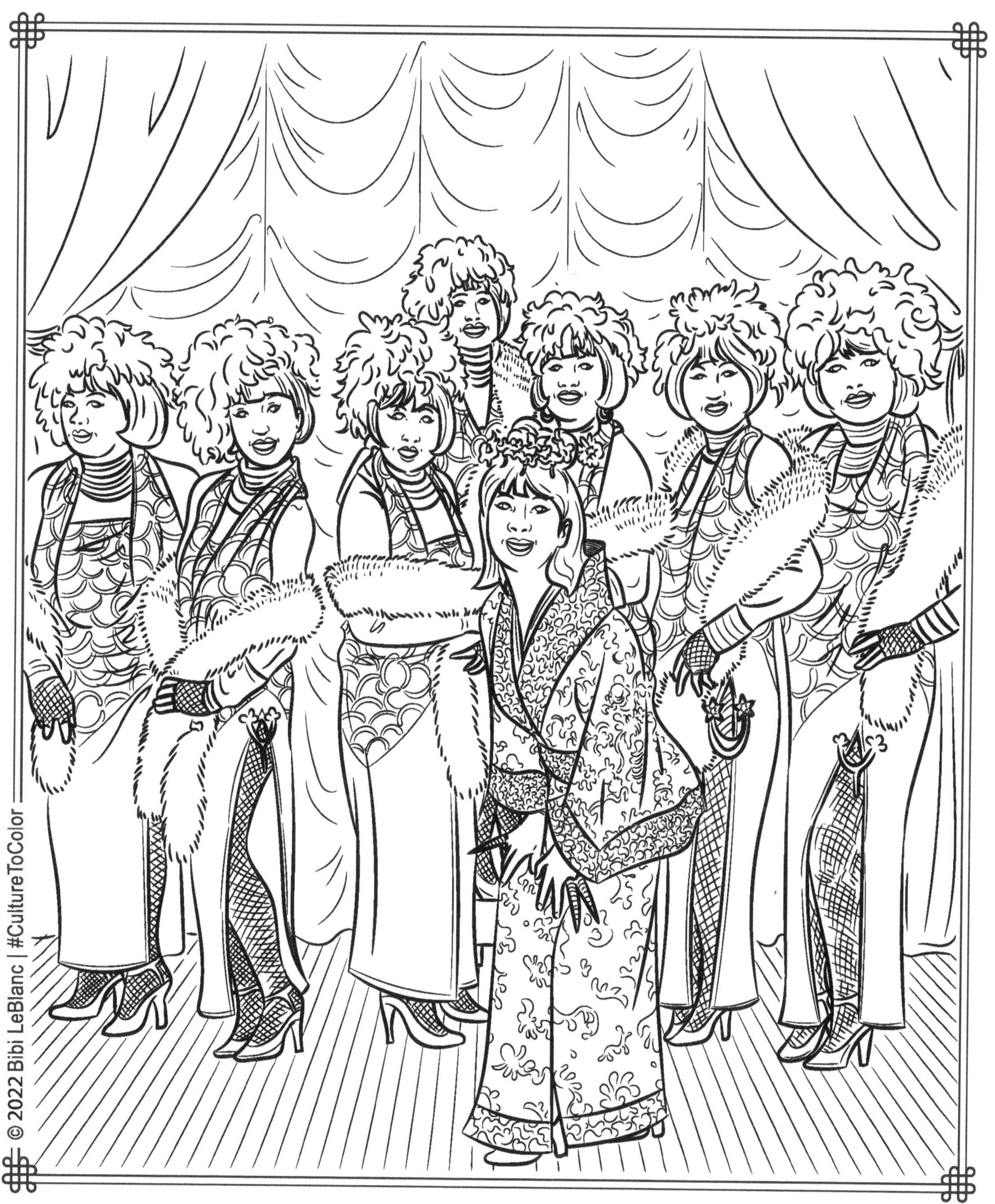

GRANT AVENUE FOLLIES

都板街鬧劇團

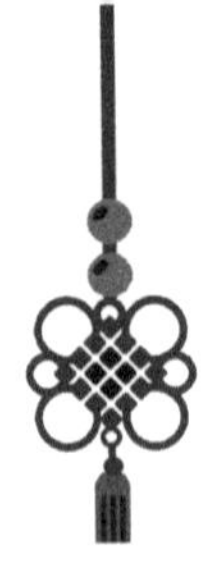

Showgirl Magic Museum
at Clarion Performing Arts Center

華聲演艺中心裡的歌舞女郎魔术博物馆

2 Waverly Place

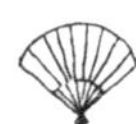

This small museum in the basement of the Clarion Performing Arts Center
is considered a local treasure. The Clarion provides education and brings entertainment
to the community celebrating music, theater, art, and poetry. Originally used for
music lessons, its downstairs space was transformed into a museum dedicated
to the vibrant nightclub scene in San Francisco Chinatown during the 1950s and '60s.

The museum's founder, Cynthia Yee, a former dancer and Miss Chinatown of 1967,
created this space to preserve the history and culture of the era. In beautiful displays,
the museum depicts the lives of the dancers of that time. Admire the
hand-embroidered costumes, ornate headdresses, wall-sized prints of dancers,
fancy jewelry, framed photos — one including Frank Sinatra — and other memorabilia
that tell stories of a glamorous past.

It's a place where young people can explore a part of Chinatown's cultural history,
and the older generations can reminisce about going out in tuxedos and
evening gowns to see live bands and dancers.

The Showgirl Magic Museum at the Clarion Performing Arts Center honors
the 20th-century Chinatown nightclub era, and is well worth a visit!

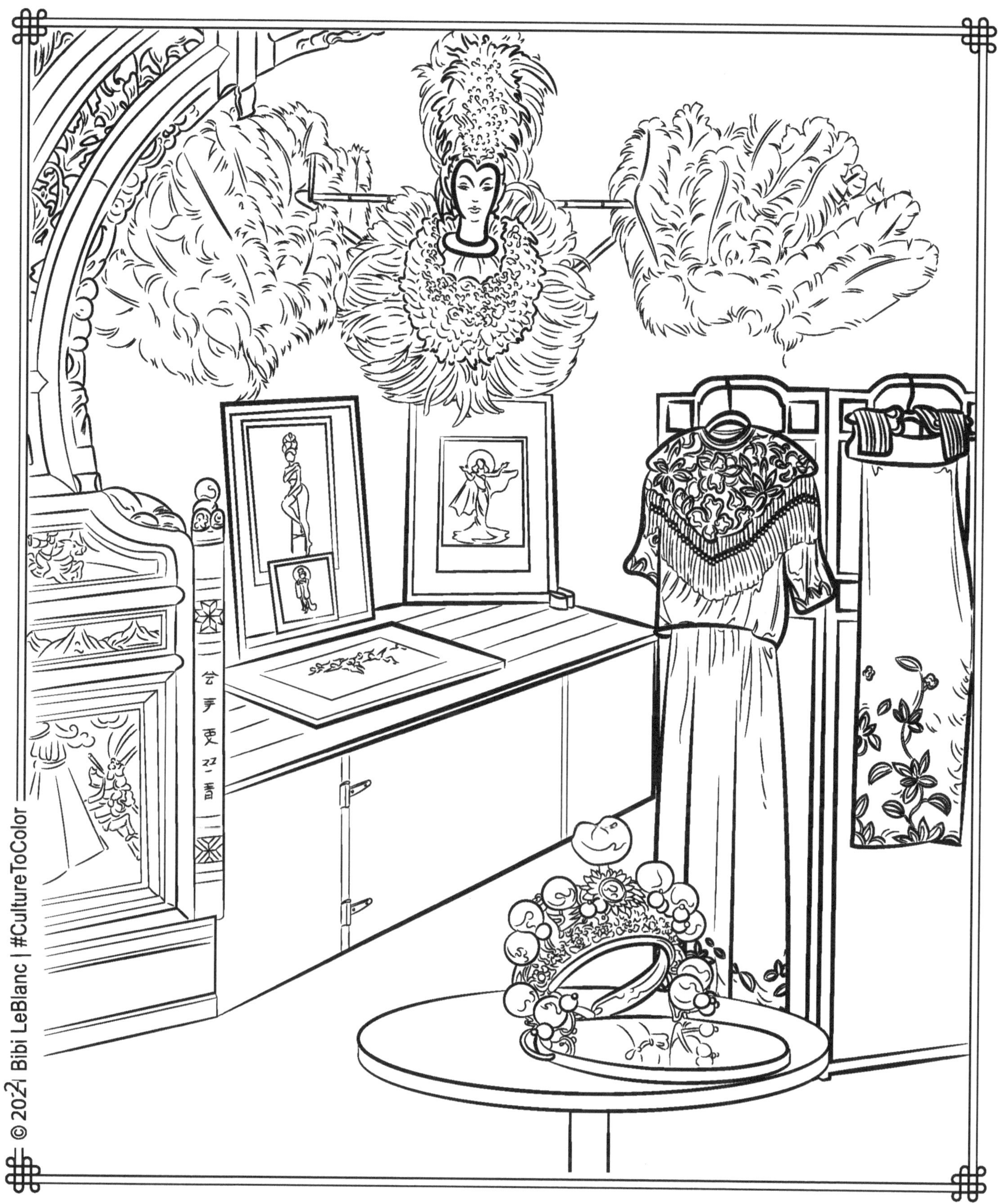

Showgirl Magic Museum
at Clarion Performing Arts Center

華聲演艺中心裡的歌舞女郎魔术博物馆

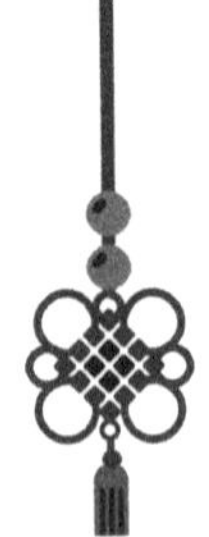

PORTSMOUTH SQUARE

花园角广场

At the heart of this bustling community is Portsmouth Square. Established in the 1800s, and named in honor of the USS Portsmouth, Portsmouth Plaza became the first public square in the city.

The square is rich in history, and includes statues, plaques, and other markers commemorating individuals, and historical events:

· A bronze plaque marks the raising of the first U.S. flag in 1846.
· California opened its first public school in 1847 adjacent to the plaza.
· A small red pagodalike structure marks the original site of the
California Star newspaper office.
· Sam Brannan, publisher of the California Star, announced
the discovery of gold in the square.
· When California became the 31st state in the Union,
the first Admission Day was celebrated here in 1850.
· A model of the Hispaniola, the ship in the novel Treasure Island, and a moving
inscription commemorate Robert Louis Stevenson, who lived here in the late 1800s.
· The Goddess of Democracy statue in the middle of the square
honors the struggle for freedom in China.

To this day, Portsmouth Square remains the vibrant center of Chinatown!
It is a popular meeting spot for locals and visitors alike! Early in the morning,
you might find locals practicing tai chi. Later in the day, the square comes alive
with groups of men and women setting up makeshift tables to play card games,
chess, and mahjong.

Portsmouth Square is a picturesque place to relax and enjoy life, observe people, and
sometimes even experience an impromptu musical performance. The square
is undergoing modifications to serve the community better.

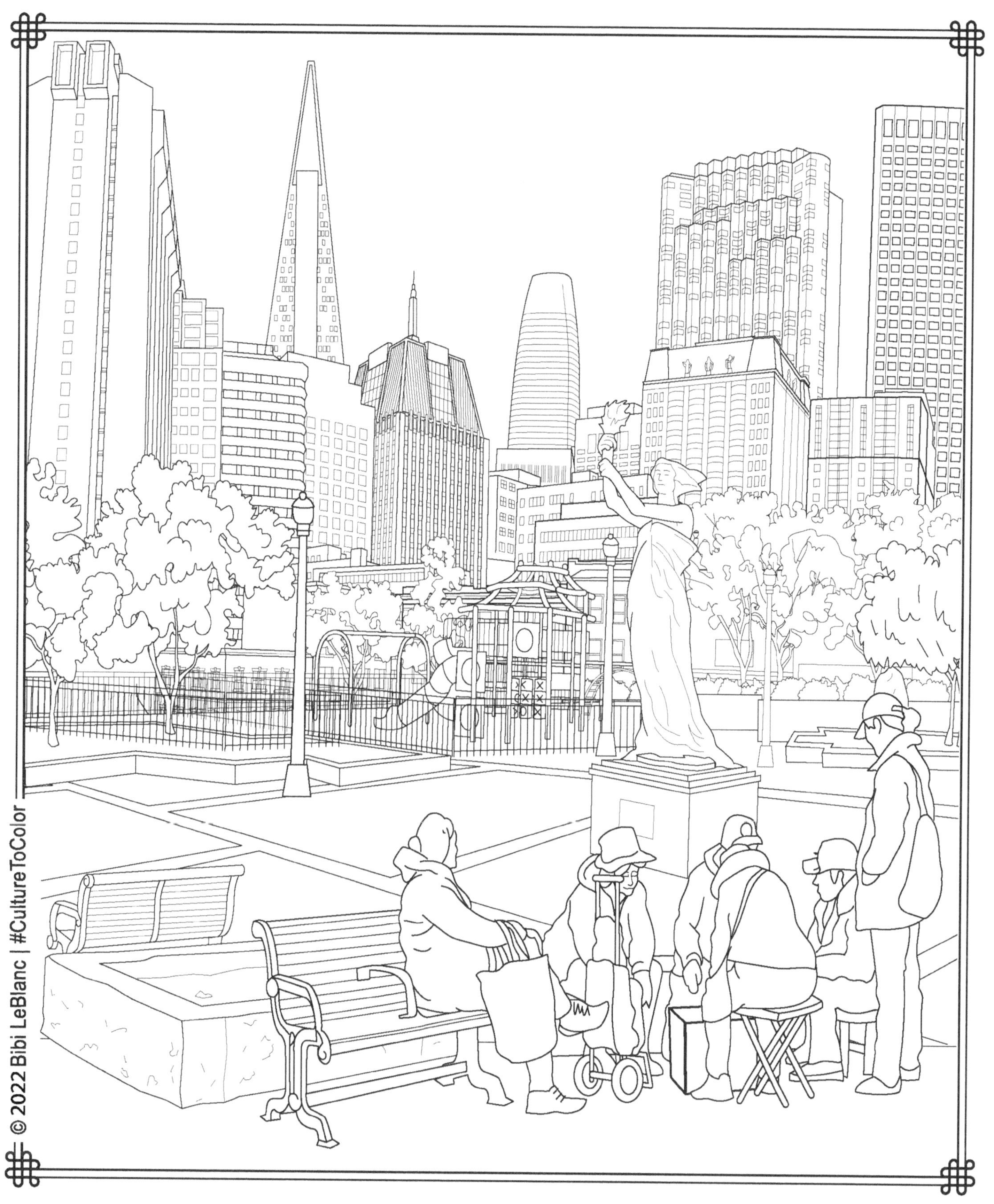

Portsmouth Square

花园角广场

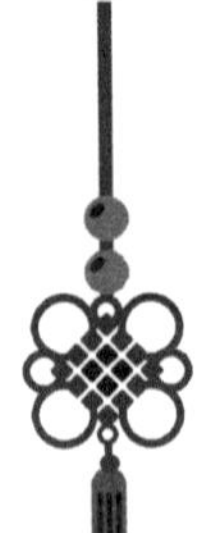

Tai Chi
太极

If you find yourself in Chinatown early in the morning, visit Portsmouth Square, where you might see people practicing the ancient martial art of tai chi.

Consisting of a series of graceful, deliberate movements, which might look easy to the observer, tai chi requires consistent practice to master. This Chinese martial art, a non-strenuous form of self-defense, is suitable for all age groups, regardless of fitness levels and agility.

According to legend, Zhang San Feng, a Taoist monk, originally developed tai chi after watching a crane and a snake fighting. He observed the bird striking out at the snake. Instead of returning the force or reacting in opposition to it, the snake avoided the crane with smooth, evasive motions. The monk then developed a series of self-defensive moves that simply required avoiding the opponent's attacks.

Today, people practice tai chi as a type of self-defense and a form of meditation. It is often referred to as a "meditation in motion." It has proved to have many health benefits, such as stress management, balance, and flexibility. Health foundations and organizations around the world use this meditative exercise in their healing programs.

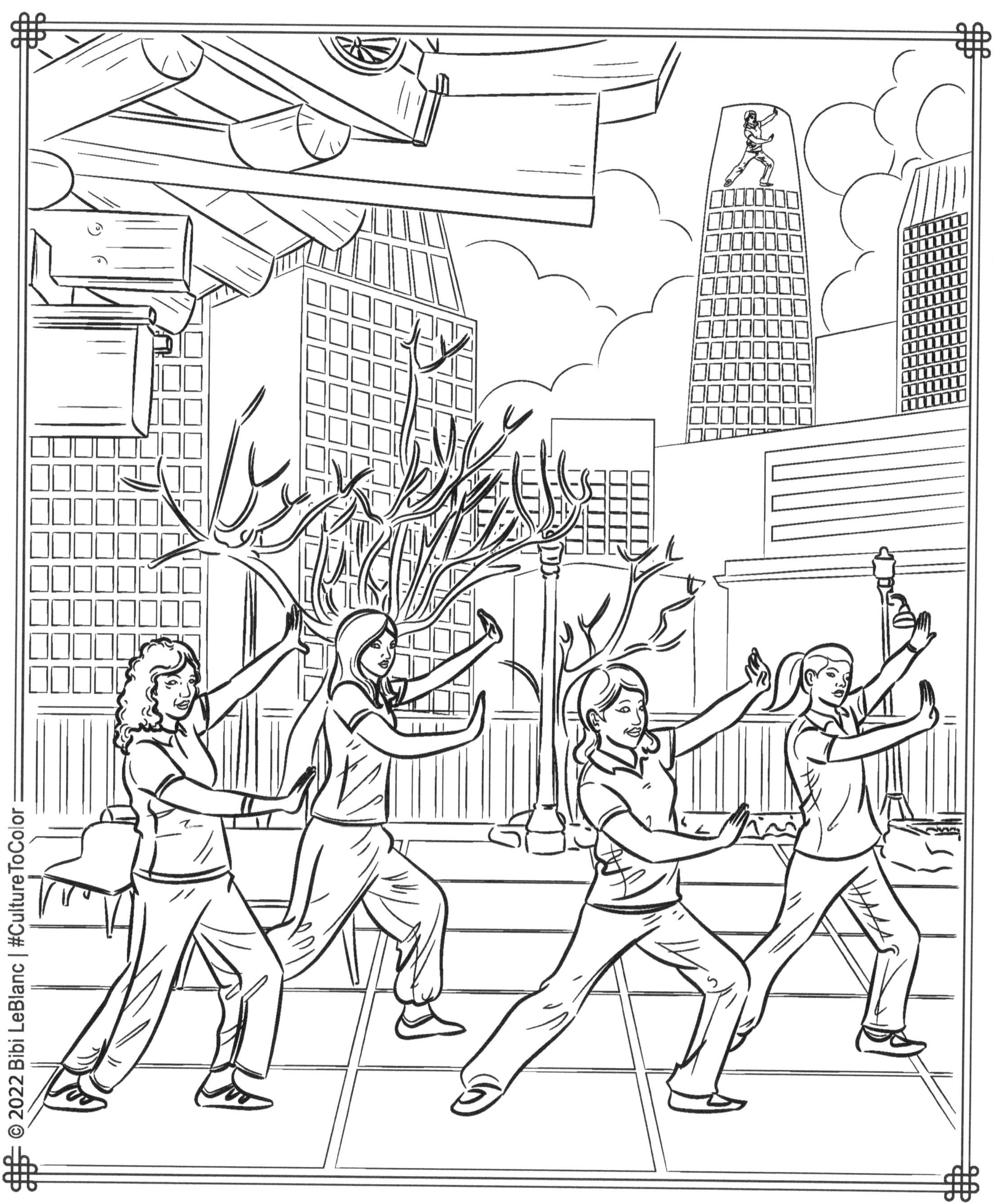

TAI CHI

太极

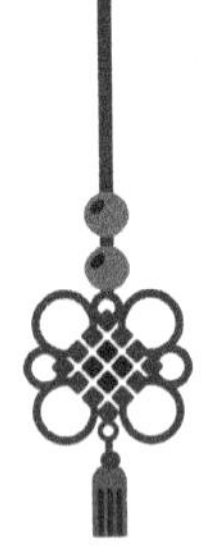

CHINESE KITES
中国风筝

"Come on, go fly a kite!"
— Albert Cheng, The Chinatown Kite Shop

Kite flying is a popular pastime in San Francisco. The cold ocean water, temperate climate, and topography produce a consistent breeze. With the Golden Gate Bridge as a backdrop, Marina Green and Crissy Field are favorite kite-flying locations in the city.

Invented in China, the first kites were built with bamboo or other light woods and paper or cloth, such as silk. The building and flying of kites is a Chinese tradition that dates back thousands of years. Designed to mimic birds in flight, kites were used initially to measure distances, calculate and record wind readings, and provide a unique way to communicate, similar to ship flags at sea.

Kites play an essential role in Chinese celebrations. The designs, colors, and symbols have different meanings and represent numerous aspects of Chinese culture. The design, size, and shape of kites vary greatly. Some are three-dimensional; others are flat. The tail can be several hundred yards long. Strings, whistles, and even lights might be attached. Chinese kites can be representations of birds, butterflies, dragonflies, flowers or mythical animals or characters, symbolic creatures, or members of the Chinese zodiac.

The passion for kite flying has spread from China to all parts of the world. Marco Polo is credited with introducing the kite to Europe. Today, elaborate kites can be seen flying in the skies throughout the world.

DID YOU KNOW?

Many consider the invention of the kite the first step in the development of the airplane. The History of Flight Pavilion at the National Air and Space Museum in Washington, D.C., displays a plaque dedicated to the Chinese kite.

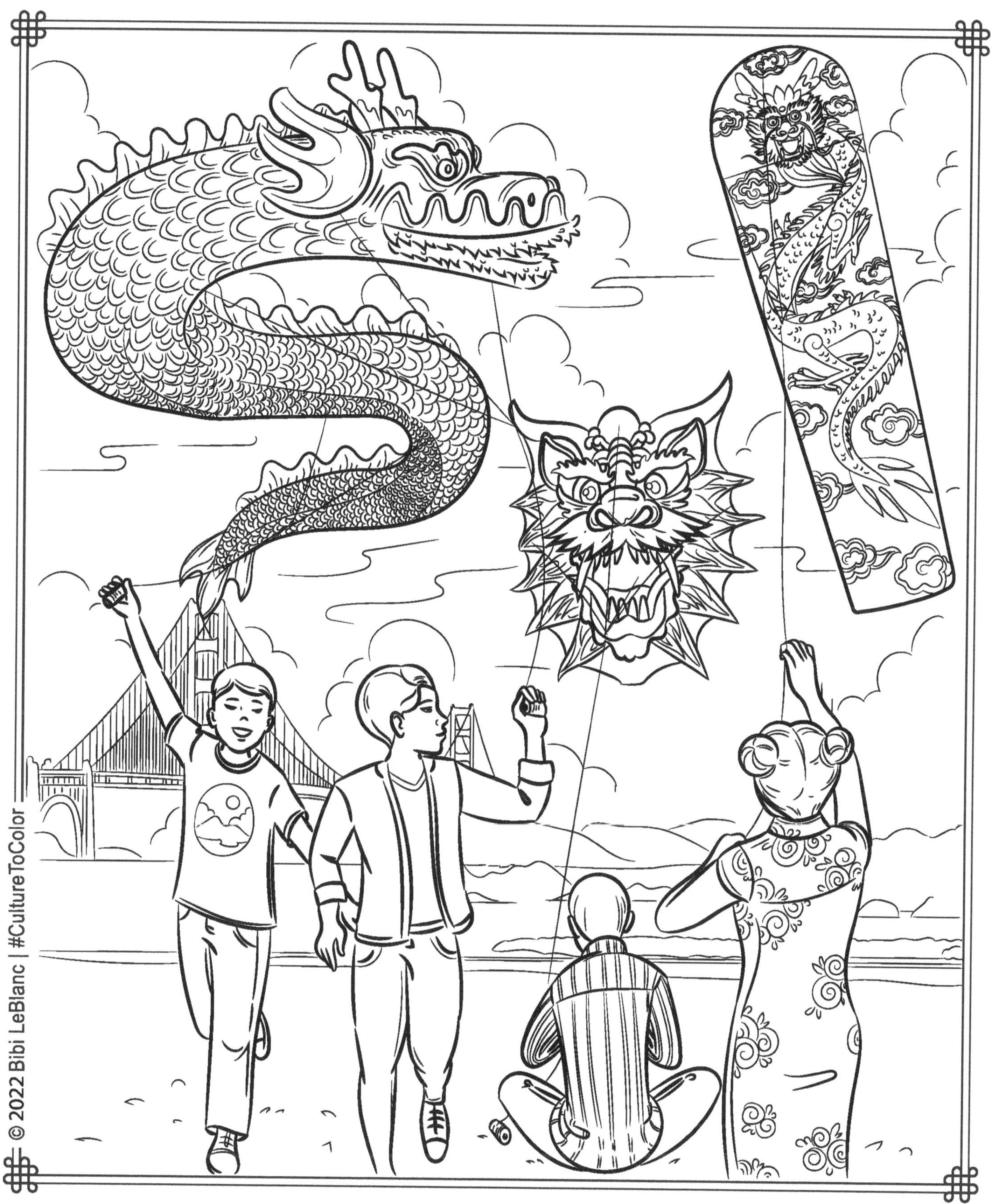

Chinese Kites

中国风筝

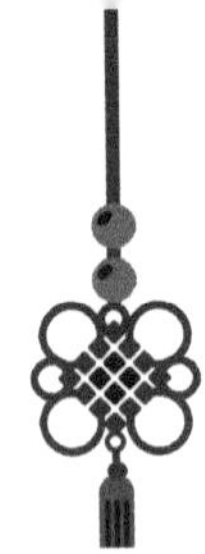

Traditional Chinese Herb Store
传统中药店

Herbs and their potential healing properties have long been part of Chinese heritage.
You can find herb stores, such as the one pictured, throughout Chinatown,
some tucked away in narrow alleys or the backs of grocery stores.

The herbalist owners of these stores have knowledge of a broad range of ailments
and illnesses, and can suggest possible remedies for most of them.
These alternative therapies might include herbs, fruits, and animal products.
You will find that these herb stores are home to kind souls who hand-pick every item
to blend an herbal mixture right before your eyes! Many of these can be ingested plain,
as teas, or prepared in a recipe given to you by the herbalist!

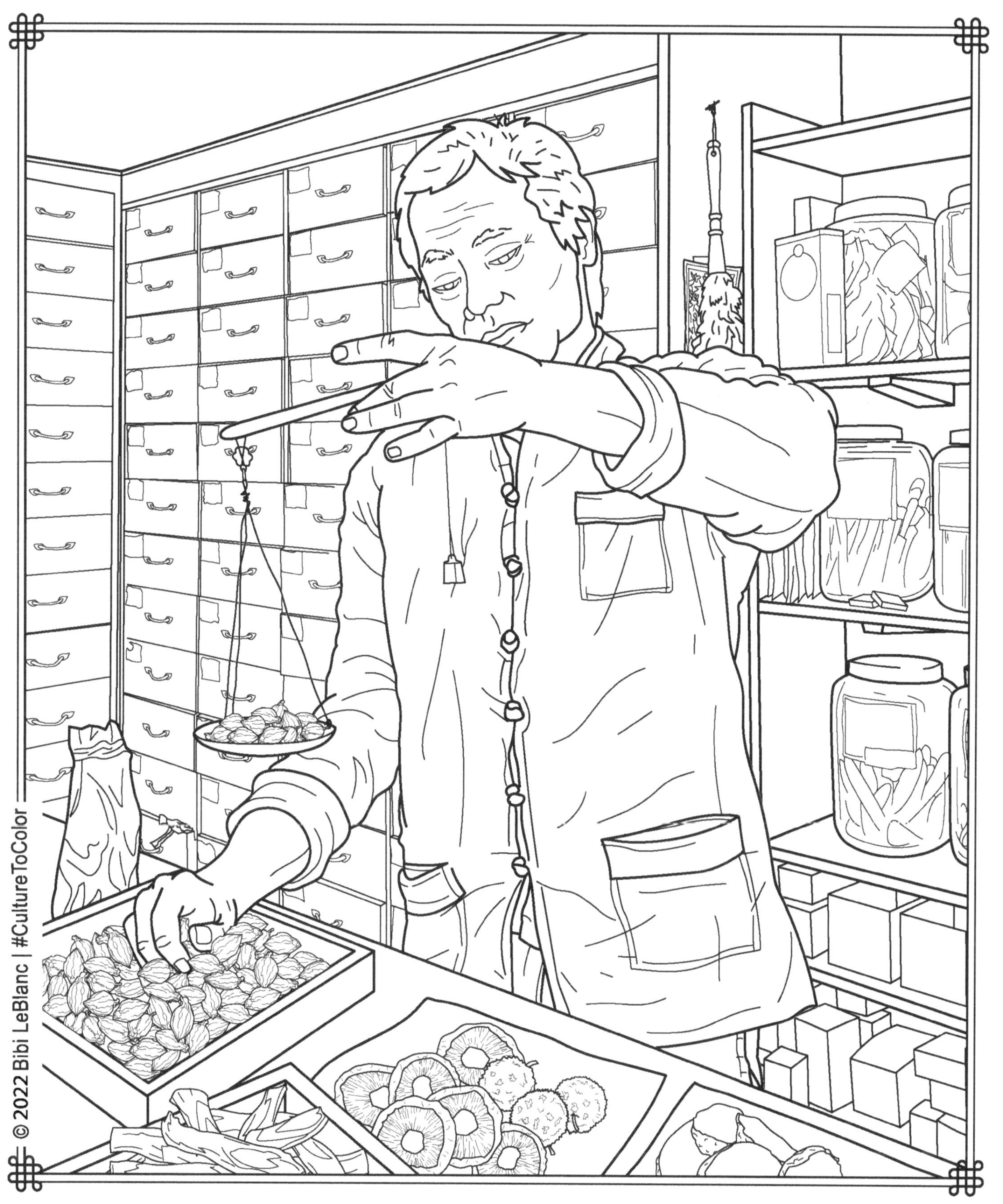

Traditional Chinese Herb Store

传统中药店

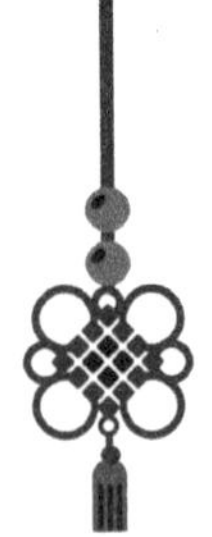

FORTUNE CATS
招财猫

Waving to you from many shop windows in Chinatown, finely dressed cat figurines with one paw raised beckon you to step inside. These good-luck charms go by many names: fortune cat, lucky cat, or money cat, to name a few. Its real name, however, is Maneki Neko, which translates to "beckoning cat."

Though originally from Japan, fortune cats are quite popular in Chinese culture. The figurines, typically seated cats wearing collars and bibs, are believed to bring good luck and fortune to their owners. Thus, they are a common sight in stores, restaurants, and other businesses.

Each cat has its unique variations, and there are specific meanings behind the differences. A fortune cat with a raised left paw brings customers and business success, while a raised right paw attracts blessings and prosperity.

Similar to the paws, the color also has a special significance. Typically, the cat's body is white, but you might find it in various colors, each offering different good fortune to its owner.

CALICO:	Invites good luck and wealth, believed to be the luckiest
WHITE:	Invites happiness and purity
BLUE:	Attracts peace and harmony
GOLD:	Brings wealth and prosperity
BLACK:	Wards off evil spirits and negative energy
GREEN:	Promises good health and increased concentration
RED OR PINK:	Attracts love and romance

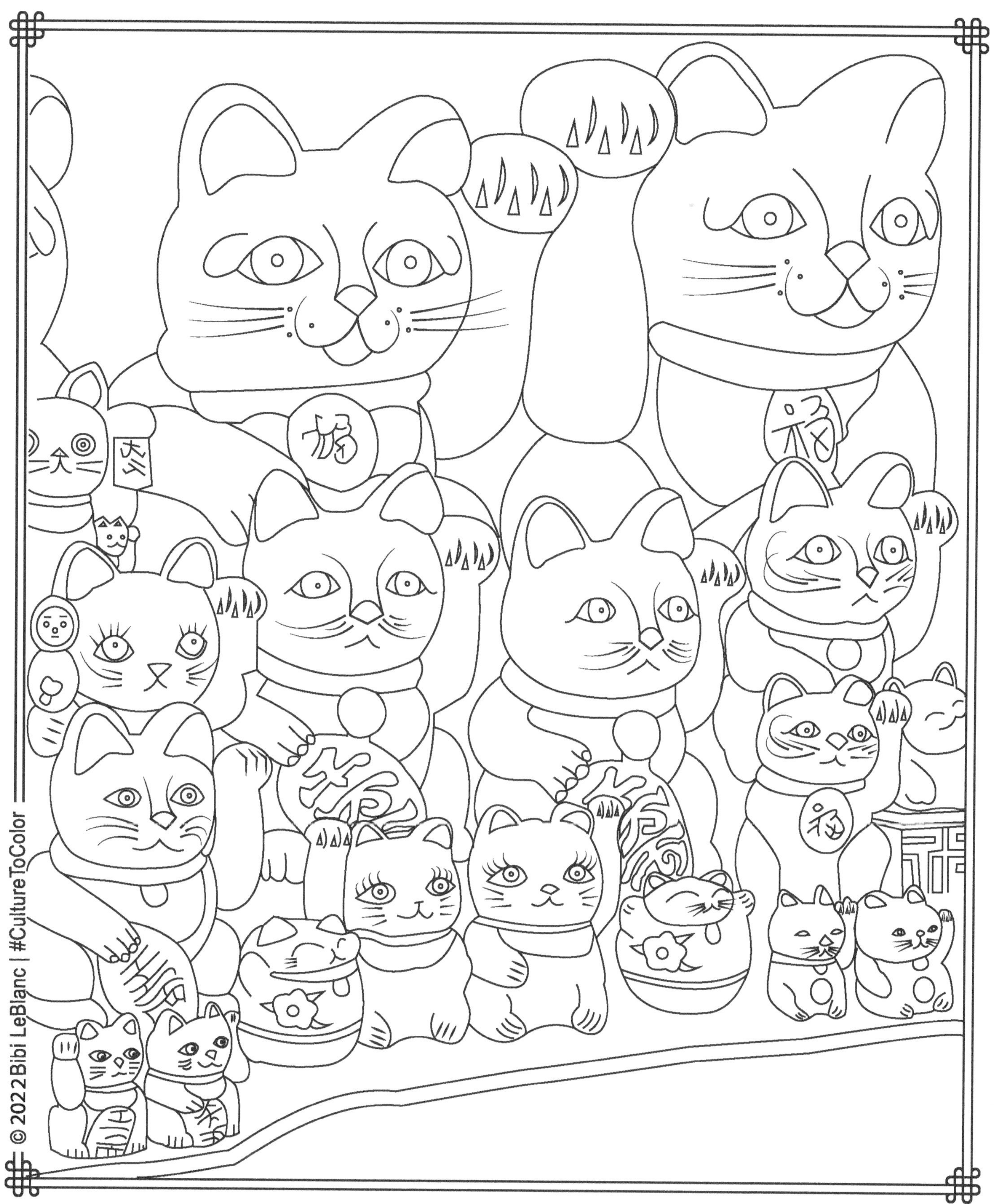

Fortune Cats

招财猫

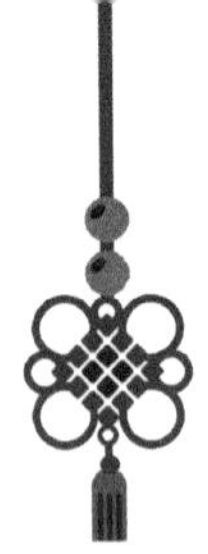

SING FAT & SING CHONG BUILDINGS
生发和生昌大厦

These two buildings, with their multitiered pagoda roofs, sit on opposite sides
of the intersection of California Street and Grant Avenue.

After the 1906 earthquake and fires destroyed most of the buildings in Chinatown,
San Francisco city officials sought to relocate the Chinese community to the outskirts
of town. But the residents immediately began re-creating their neighborhood, and
the Sing Fat and Sing Chong buildings were among the first structures erected
after the earthquake. They incorporated traditional Chinese architectural features,
and inspired unique designs and decorative elements for many other
Chinatown buildings.

The Sing Fat and Sing Chong buildings have become iconic landmarks and
are synonymous with San Francisco Chinatown. They remain two of the
most photographed sights in the city.

FUN FACT

As you meander through Chinatown, you will see hundreds of red lanterns
strung across the streets. They symbolize happiness, luck, and prosperity.
Historically, Chinese people displayed red lanterns when family visited.

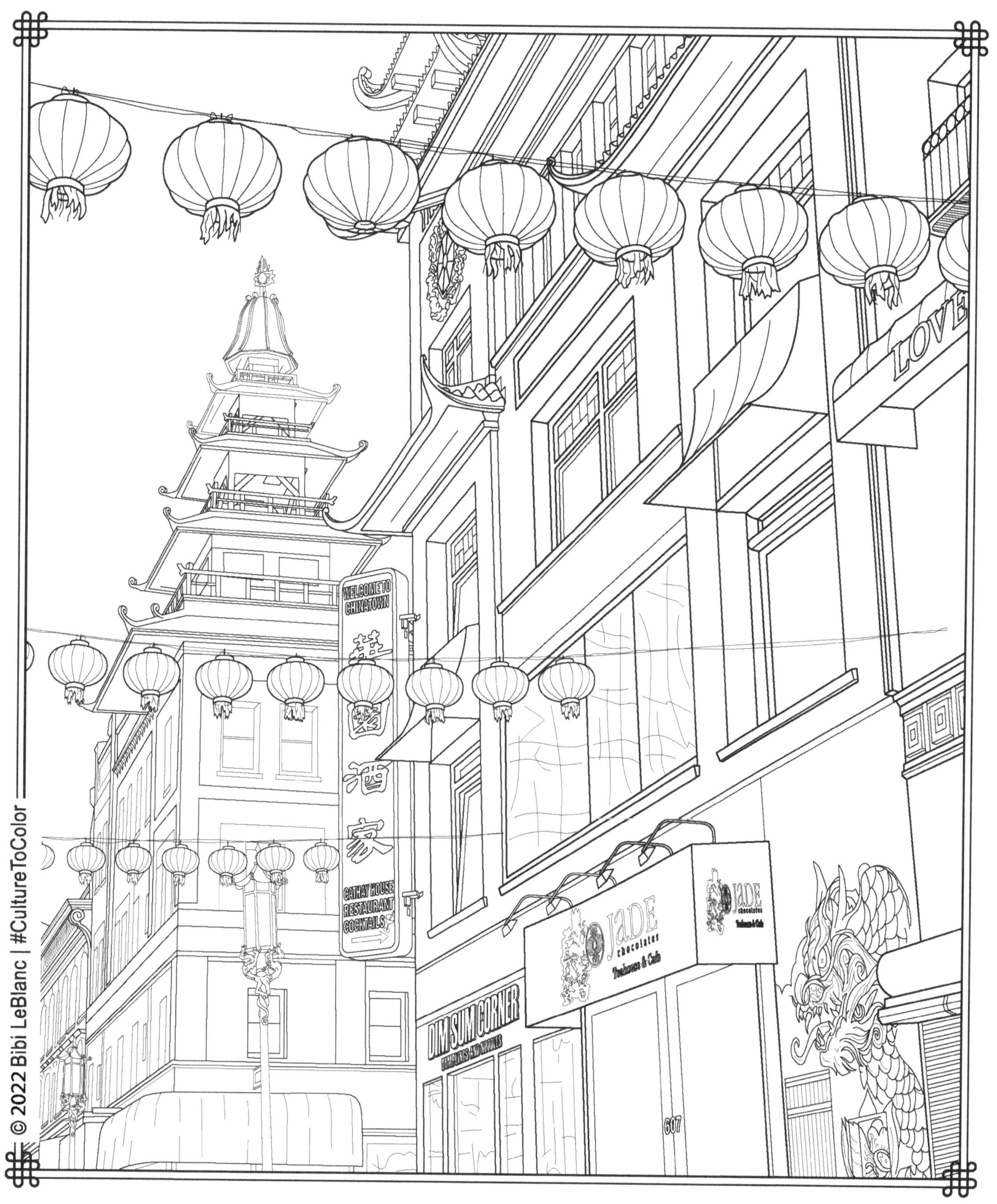

Sing Fat & Sing Chong Buildings

生发和生昌大厦

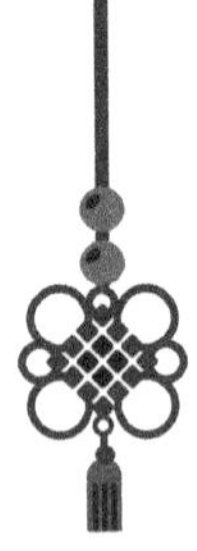

Bian Lian
The Ancient Art of Face Changing
变脸—古代的变脸艺术

Rarely seen in the United States, the mysterious art of Bian Lian — face changing —
is another example of the unique Chinese culture! Its roots are found in
Sichuan opera and can be traced back about 300 years. Bian Lian has long
been a closely guarded secret of Chinese performers, and is a skill families would
pass down only to their heirs.

During a Bian Lian performance, the artist changes elaborately designed masks
with astonishing speed using precisely choreographed moves. With the wave of a fan,
a swish of the cape, or a quick turn, a new mask appears. The masks, often self-made,
convey varying moods and emotions. A skilled performer can change up to 10 masks
in under 20 seconds! This rapid swapping of masks is an astonishing feat
that few have mastered!

The face changers in San Francisco Chinatown enthrall audiences during holiday
festivities and other special occasions. It's a special treat, and fascinates young
and old alike.

Fun Fact

One of the legendary tales surrounding Bian Lian tells the story
of a Chinese Robin Hood who changed his appearance to confuse
his pursuers and escape.

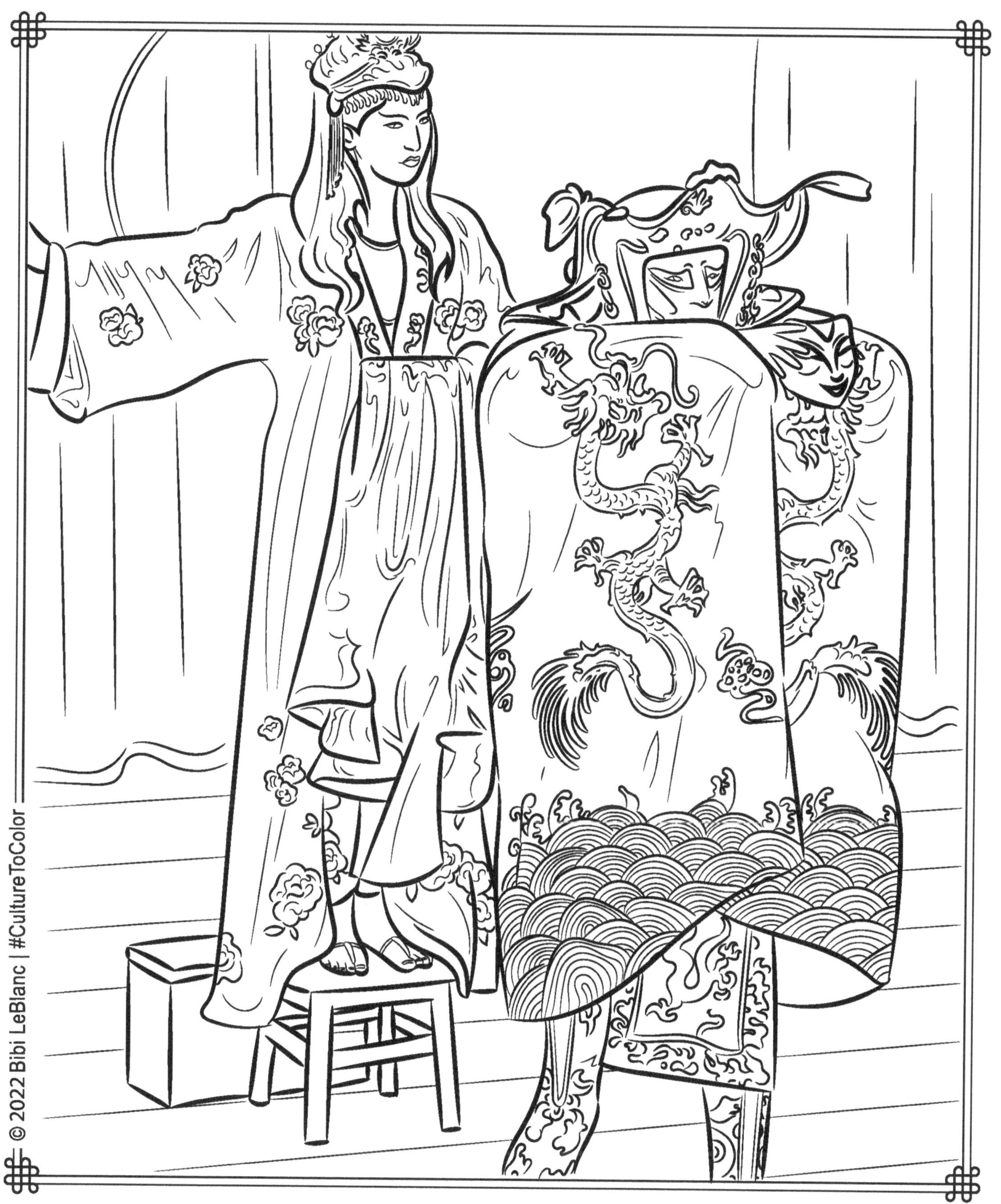

BIAN LIAN - THE ANCIENT ART OF FACE CHANGING

变脸—古代的变脸艺术

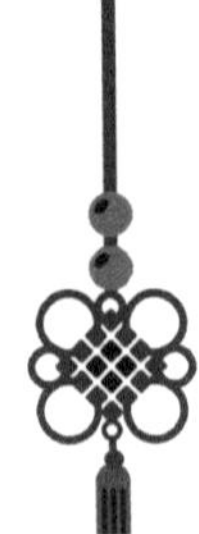

STOCKTON STREET MARKETS
市德頓街市场

Walk the crowded sidewalks past boxes of dried fish, displays of exotic produce, and restaurant windows festooned with roasted ducks, and take in the sounds and smells for an intense immersion into Chinatown.

Among the great variety of shopping opportunities in Chinatown, the Stockton Street produce and live markets offer some of the most intriguing shops to browse. With produce stands, fish markets, and bakeries, this is where most locals, and even many from outside of Chinatown, buy the freshest and most economical groceries.

Found just one block west of Grant Avenue, Stockton Street offers a unique glimpse into life off-the-beaten-tourist-path in Chinatown. You could spend an entire day wandering in and out of stores trying to identify the plethora of unique food items. What makes the adventure more challenging is that the signs in the shops are often in Chinese, but shopkeepers will answer any questions you might have.

Here is your chance to try some durian, salted duck eggs, Buddha's hand, dehydrated shrimp, and dragon fruit, to name a few of the exotic offerings.

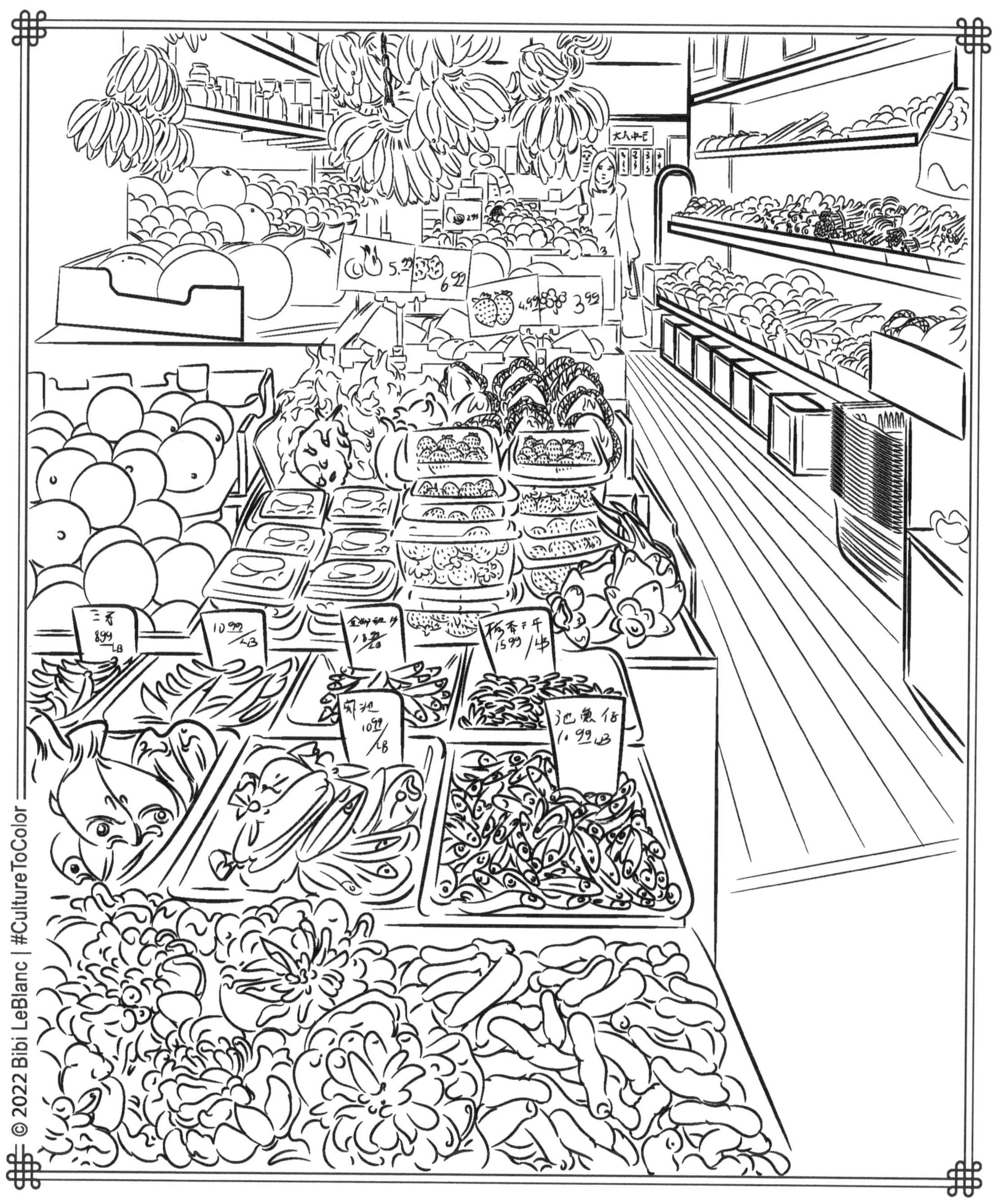

Stockton Street Markets

市德頓街市场

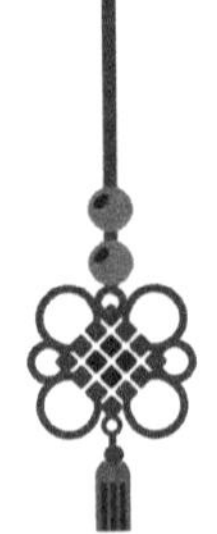

WOKS

炒锅

"A wok is like a woman. The older, the better!"
— Tane Chan, The Wok Shop

First invented in China during the Han dynasty over 2,000 years ago, the wok
is one of the most common cooking utensils in Chinese cuisine. The word
"wok" is derived from the Cantonese word for "cooking pot."

The round-bottom of a wok distributes the heat more evenly than does a saucepan,
allowing the ingredients to cook in less time. The long handle and high walls
allow for food to be tossed easily.

A wok can be used for much more than just stir-fry. You can steam, pan and deep-fry,
boil, braise, sear, smoke, and stew your food! It is a versatile cooking tool, and
has become popular around the world.

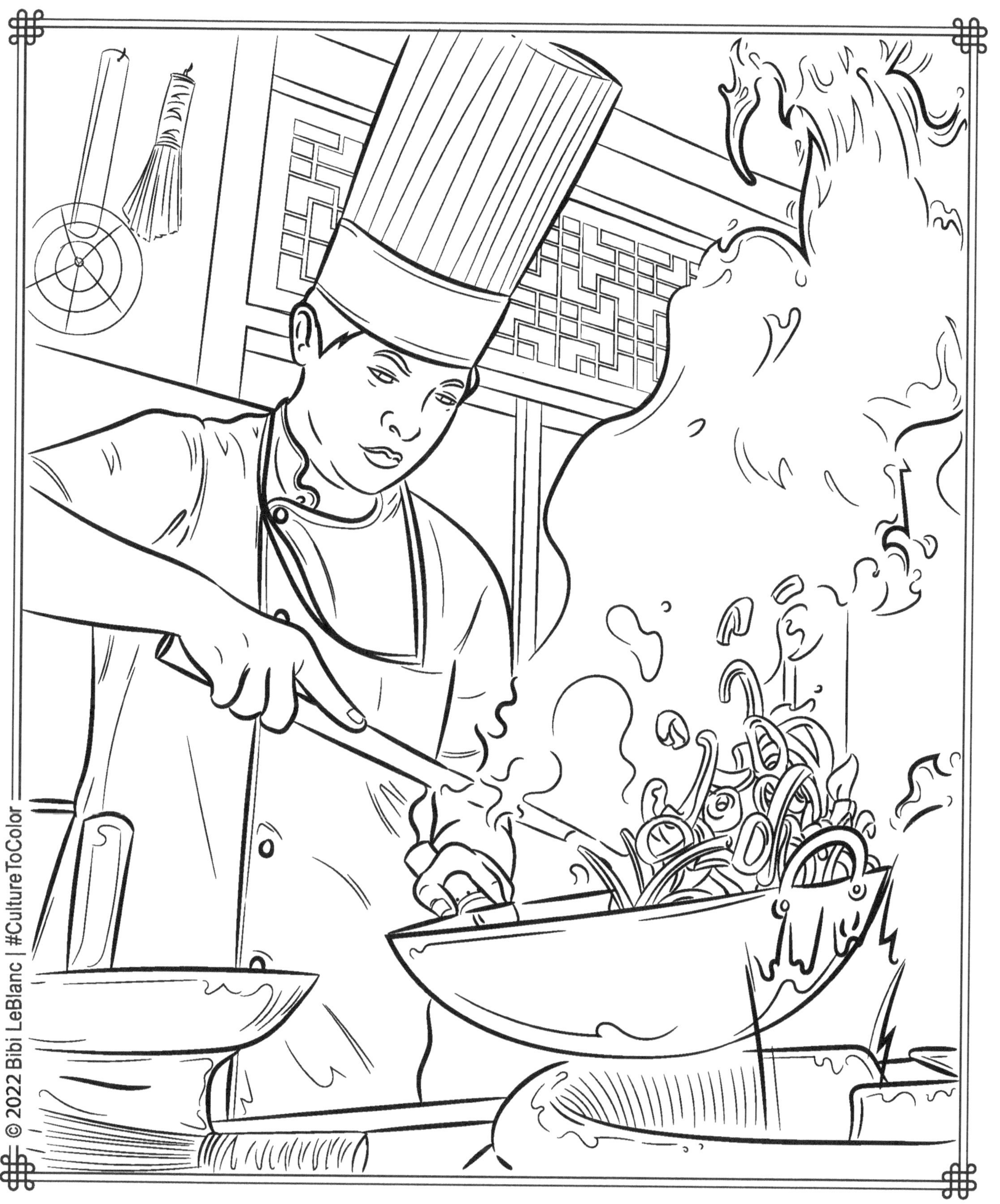

Woks

炒锅

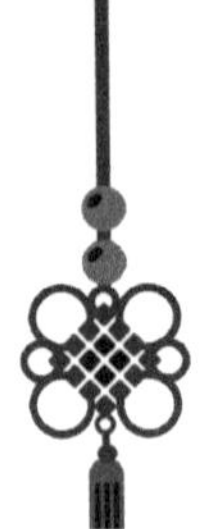

Dim Sum

点心

Be sure to get a taste of Chinatown while you're here! A great way to experience a wide variety of flavors is to try dim sum.

Dim sum originated in 10th-century China when commercial travelers stopped at teahouses for tea and small meals. As this practice became more popular, influences and traditions from different regions broadened the varieties available.

Traditionally enjoyed for breakfast or lunch, dim sum includes steamed or fried dumplings, buns, and rice noodle rolls. Fillings range from savory — chicken, pork, shrimp, prawns, vegetables — to sweet, such as pineapple, water chestnuts, and taro. Since dim sum is prepared in small portions of three or four, it is ideal for sharing and experiencing an array of textures and flavors.

If you want to try dim sum, consider any of these popular options

Har Gow	Shrimp Dumplings
Shao Mai	Steamed Dumplings with pork, shrimp or both
Lo Mai Gai	Rice wrapped in lotus leaf
Cha Siu Bao	Barbecue Pork Bun
Yu Tou Gao	Taro Cake with mashed taro, shrimp or pork, mushrooms
Bo Luo Bao	Pineapple Bun

Dim sum means "to touch the heart" – try some and discover the reason for yourself!

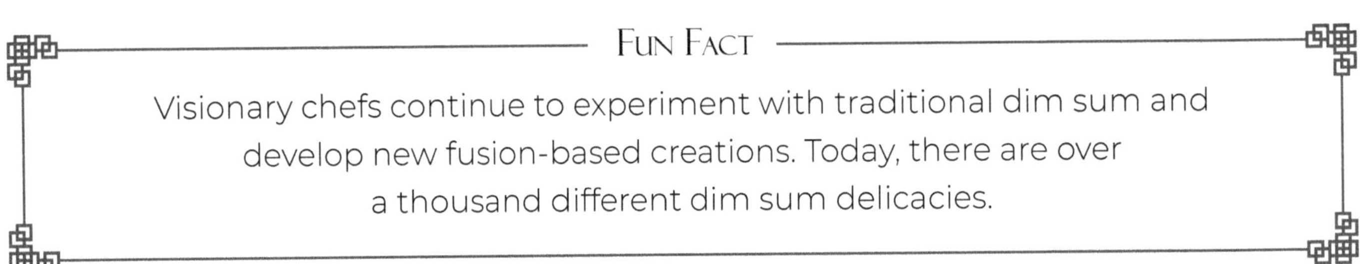

Fun Fact

Visionary chefs continue to experiment with traditional dim sum and develop new fusion-based creations. Today, there are over a thousand different dim sum delicacies.

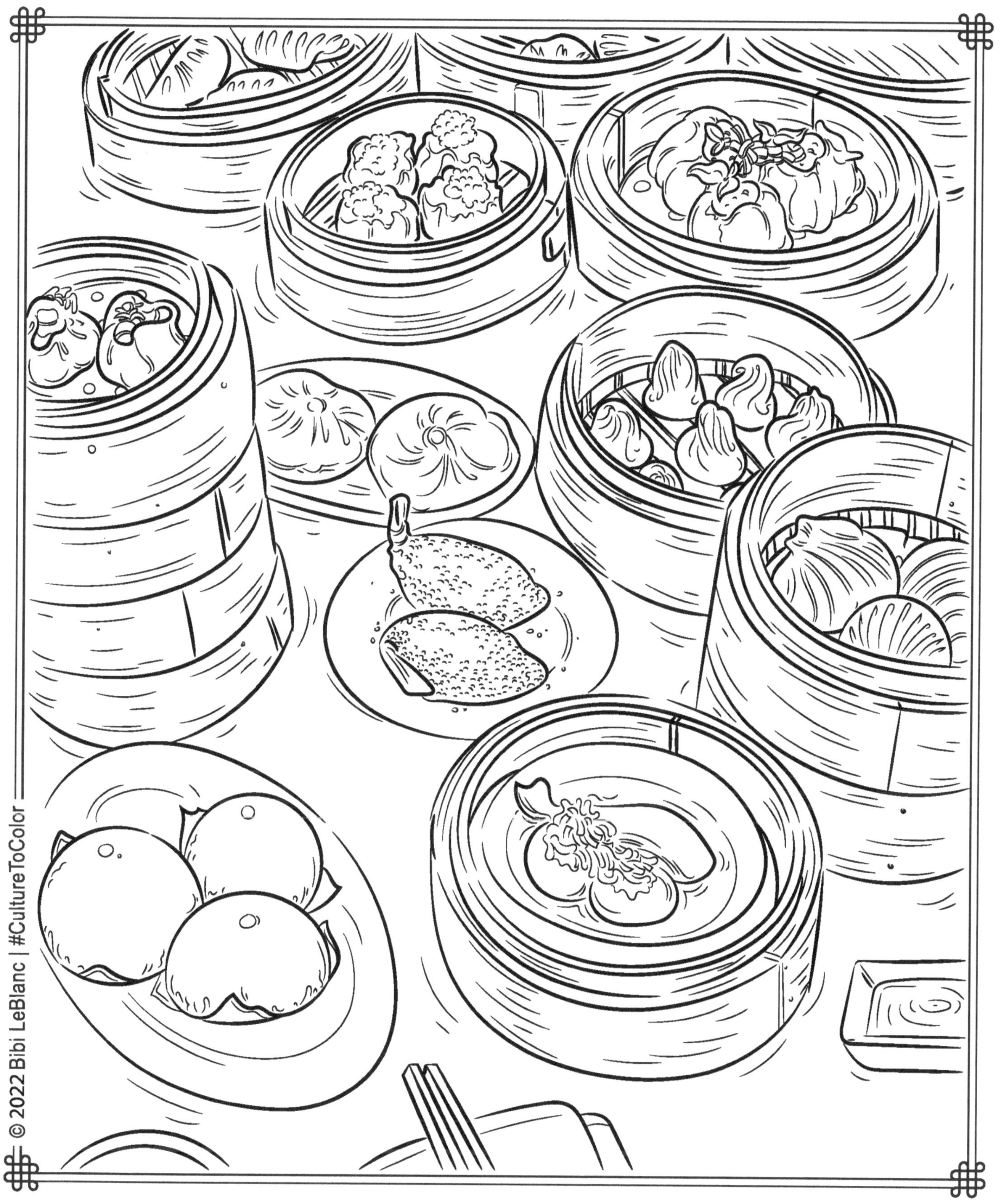

Dim Sum

点心

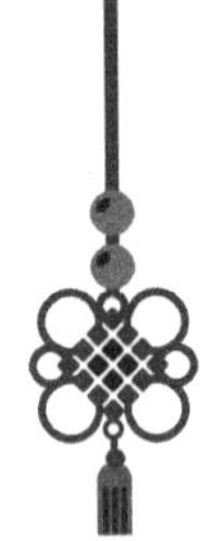

Traditional & Modern
传统与现代

Corner of Grant Avenue & Clay Street

Pause for a moment as you walk through Chinatown and note the visual effect of traditional and modern styles side by side. This contrast can be stunning and thought-provoking.

One such example can be found at the intersection of Grant Avenue and Clay Street, where replicas of the famous Terra-Cotta Warriors add dimension to the warrior mural on the side of the building. Magnifying the allure of this scene are the Transamerica building in the background and a dragon streetlamp in the forefront, creating a unique photo opportunity.

Dragon Streetlamps
The original dragon streetlamps were created for the 1925 celebration of the San Francisco Diamond Jubilee, commemorating the 75th anniversary of California's statehood. The Downtown Merchants Association, Chinese Chamber of Commerce, and San Francisco Diamond Jubilee Festival raised funds for the lamps. They were installed along Grant Avenue, making it one of the best-lit streets in the city at the time.

The Terra-Cotta Warriors
In 1974, farmers in China discovered an ancient tomb with thousands of warrior and horse sculptures in full battle armor. Each of the statues has individual features and clothing. They were buried with Qin Shi Huang, the first emperor of China, to protect him in his afterlife. This mural was painted, and the Terra-Cotta Warrior replicas were placed on the building to honor this discovery.

Transamerica Building
The Transamerica Pyramid is a San Francisco landmark and was once the tallest skyscraper west of Chicago. The white quartz building with more than 3,600 windows is visible from many corners in San Francisco's historic Chinatown.

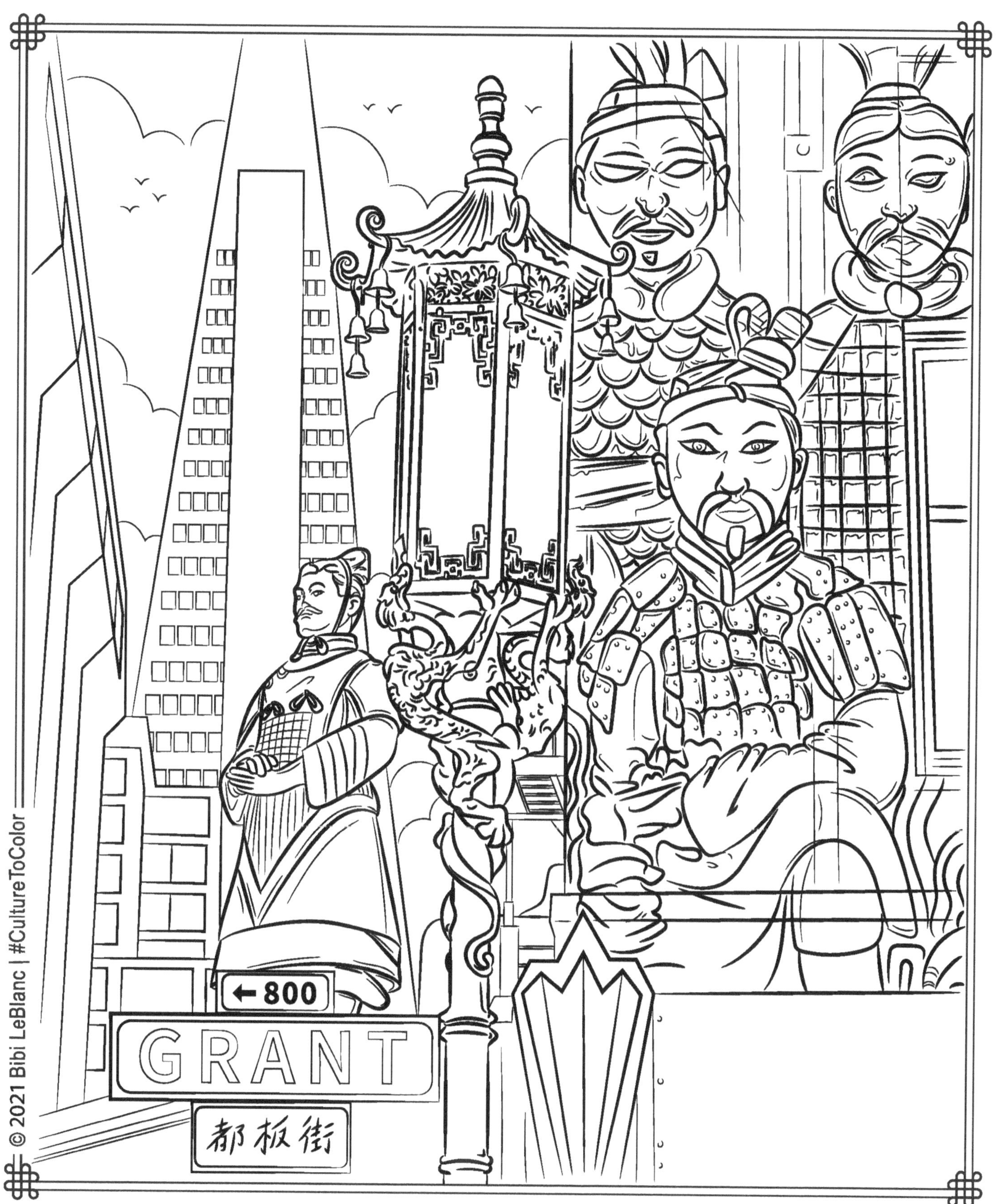

Traditional & Modern

传统与现代

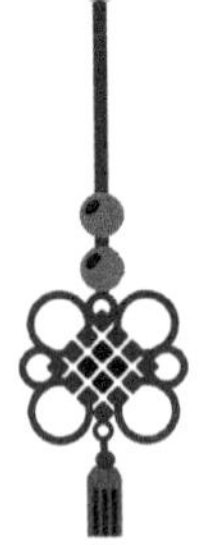

CHINESE CHESS
中国象棋

During your visit to Chinatown, you might encounter a group of people gathered around two players engaged in a game of Chinese chess. Traditionally played at teahouses, this strategic board game is an important part of Chinese culture and is considered an ancient art.

Xiangqi, Chinese chess, is also called "elephant chess." Besides elephants, the pieces include soldiers, horses, chariots, guards, cannons, and a palace. In ancient times, the game pieces were made of ivory, metal, or porcelain coins; today, they are usually wood or plastic. The game is typically played on a wooden board, though you might also see it played on a piece of paper or cardboard.

Like Western or international chess, the goal is to use your pieces to put your opponent's general (king) into checkmate. Despite the similarities, there are significant differences in the movements of the game pieces.

Played by old and young, the game is popular around the globe as a way to stimulate the brain, socialize, or play competitively. If you are intrigued, you can find game sets, from simple to elaborate, in many shops in Chinatown.

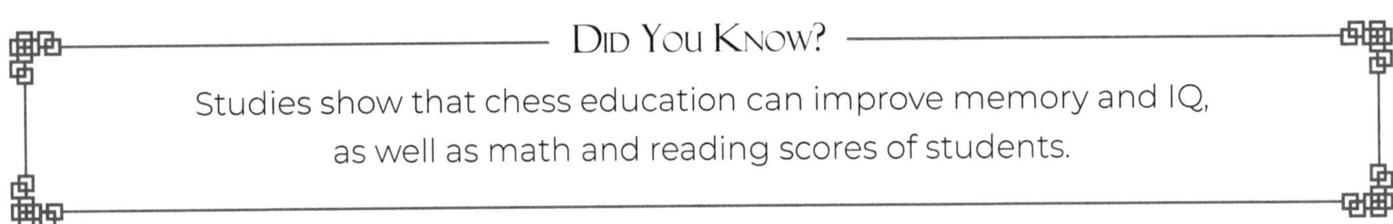

DID YOU KNOW?
Studies show that chess education can improve memory and IQ,
as well as math and reading scores of students.

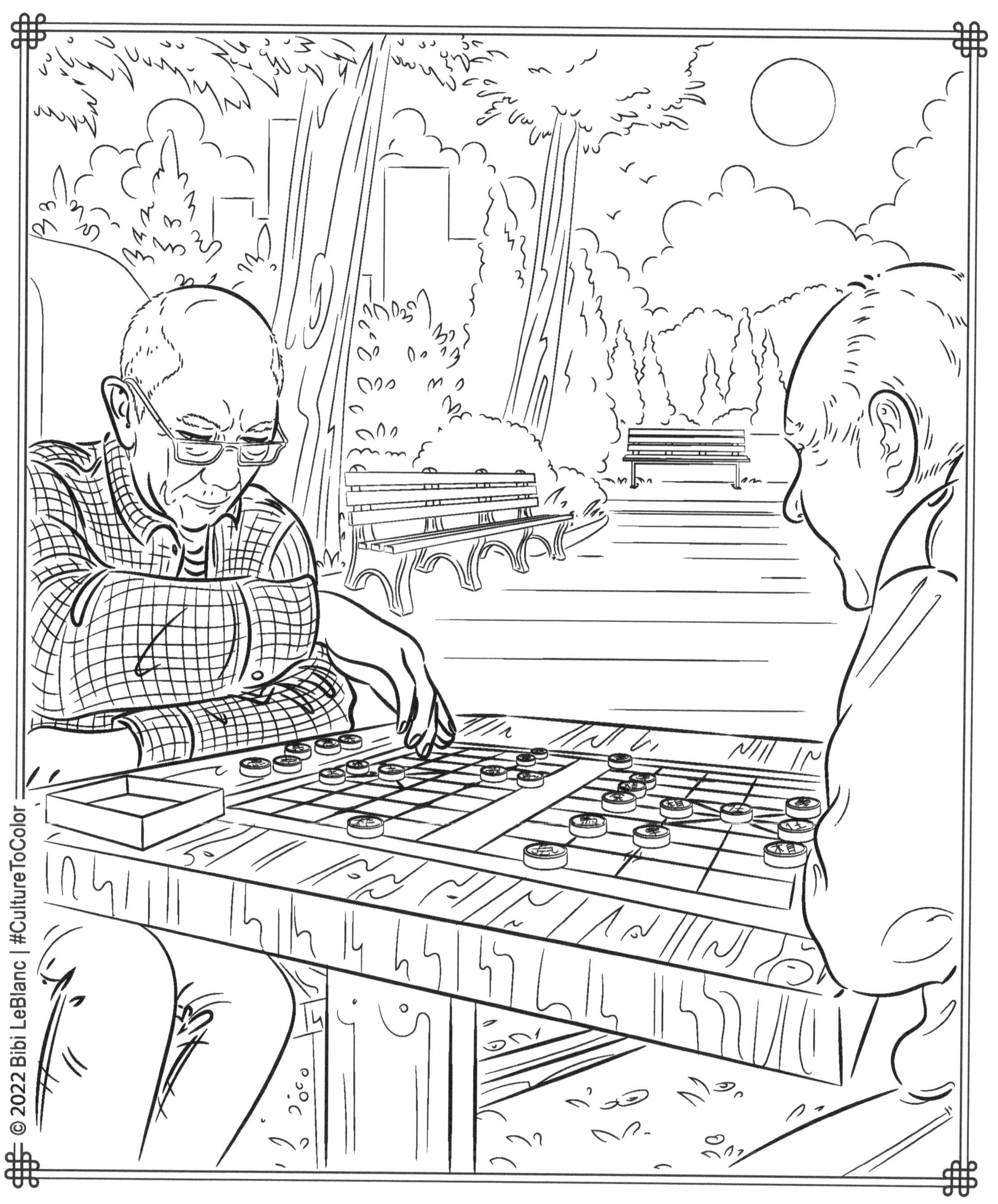

Chinese Chess

中国象棋

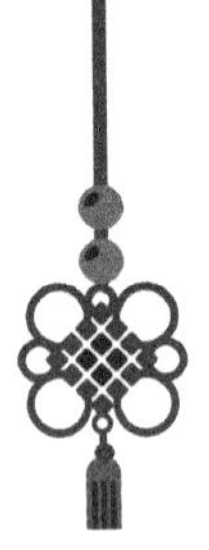

WILLIE "WOO WOO" WONG PLAYGROUND & CLUBHOUSE

黃顯護游乐场

830 Sacramento Street

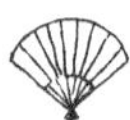

The Willie "Woo Woo" Wong Playground is a favorite destination used by residents and visitors of all ages.

Opened in 1927, this well-loved playground served as the training ground for young Willie Wong. Even though he was only 5'5" tall, he became one of the best Chinese American basketball players in the 1940s and '50s. He competed for different all-star teams and, ultimately, the University of San Francisco, where he is a member of the school's basketball hall of fame. He earned the nickname "Woo Woo" because his fans shouted "Woo! Woo!" every time he scored. In 2006, the playground was renamed to honor his contributions to the community and the game of basketball.

Chinatown residents shaped the recent redesign of the park and clubhouse. Today, this multilevel playground in the heart of Chinatown includes a rooftop basketball court and a playground with custom-designed water dragon and phoenix play structures and sand areas.

The clubhouse, with its extensive community recreation center and indoor gym, is on the lower level. Some of Willie "Woo, Woo" Wong's trophies are on display here.

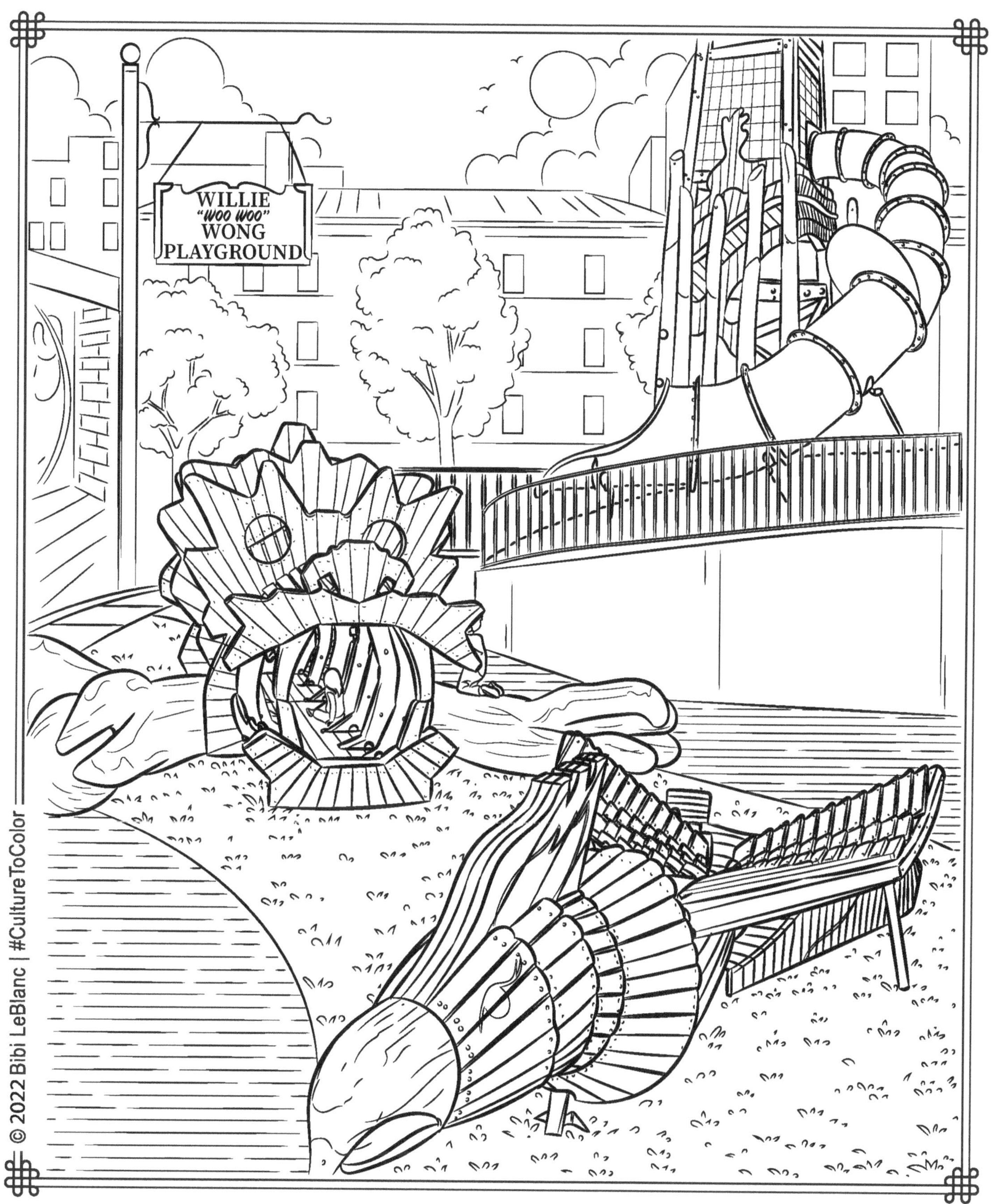

Willie "Woo Woo" Wong
Playground & Clubhouse

黃顯護游乐场

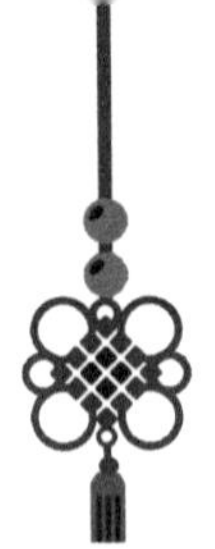

GREAT STAR THEATER
大明星戲院

636 Jackson Street

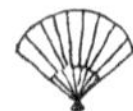

Originally named the Great China Theater, this historic venue opened as one of the first theaters in Chinatown in 1925. In its early days, it showcased Cantonese opera. In 1940, a projection booth and screen were added so that Chinese movies could be shown. People still have fond memories of watching Hong Kong kung-fu movies here as children. Over the years, other types of performances were added, including circus-themed shows and musicals. It was renamed the Great Star Theater circa 1960.

To preserve this iconic theater and its history, the new owners completed extensive renovations in 2021. Re-opening this historic theater creates new opportunities by bringing the technology and art communities together to create and produce theater. Local and international artists bring performances in a variety of genres to this stage, including ballet, cabaret, magic, Chinese opera, and movies.

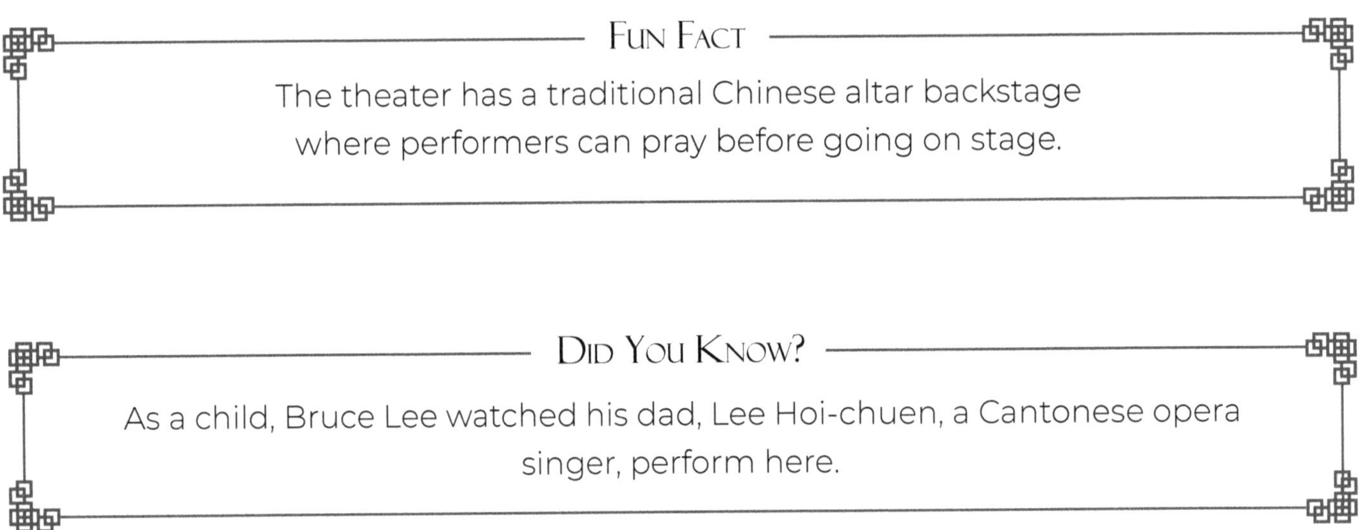

FUN FACT

The theater has a traditional Chinese altar backstage
where performers can pray before going on stage.

DID YOU KNOW?

As a child, Bruce Lee watched his dad, Lee Hoi-chuen, a Cantonese opera
singer, perform here.

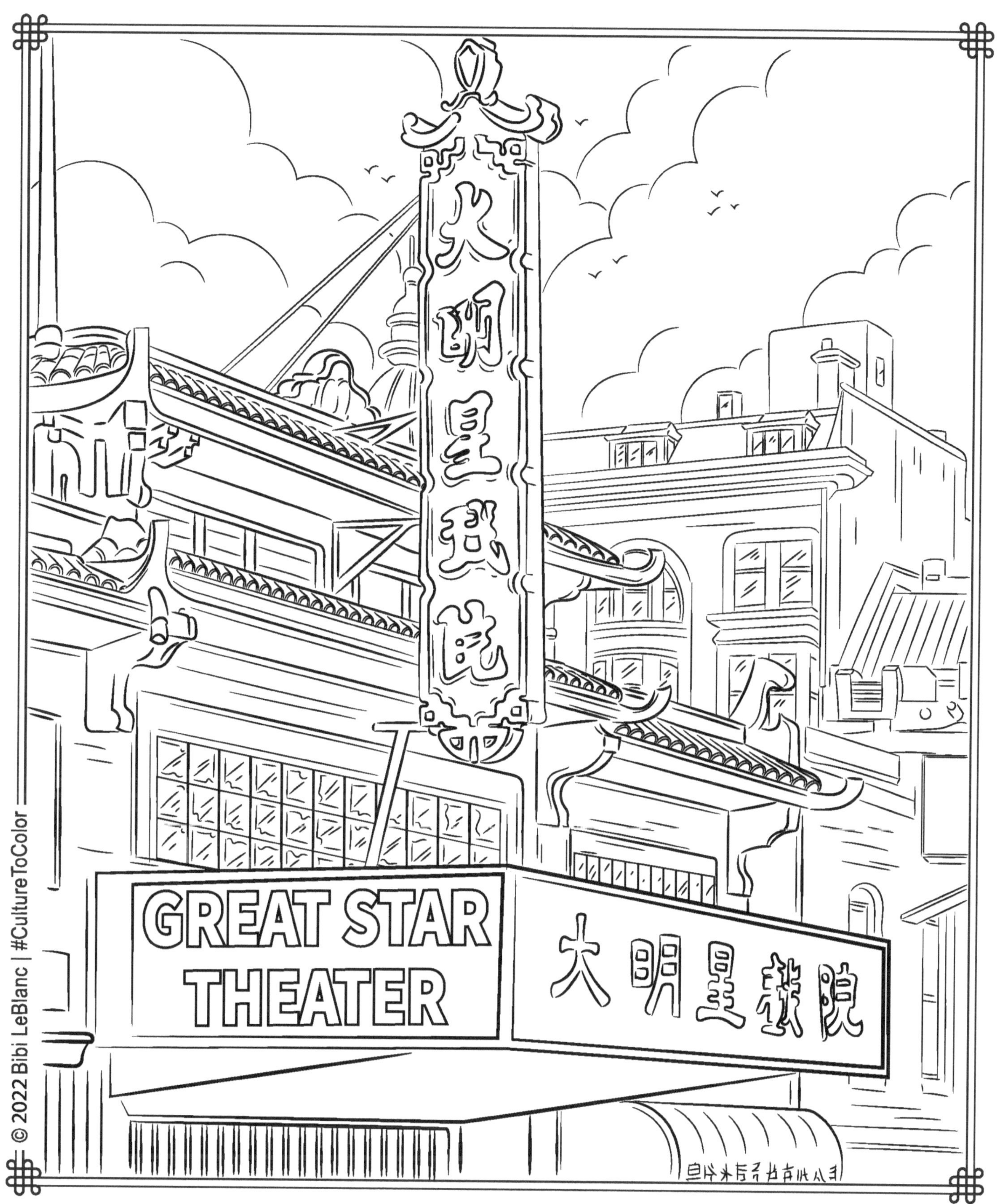

GREAT STAR THEATER

大明星戲院

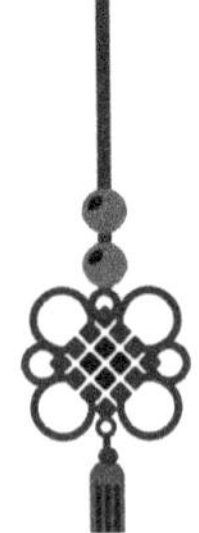

STREET LIFE
街头生活

The streets of Chinatown are full of pleasant surprises. Follow the sounds
of familiar tunes played on unfamiliar instruments to find street musicians
performing American favorites on Chinese instruments, a truly unusual experience!

. . . or end up at the Eastern Bakery, the oldest bakery in town. The long lines are
worth the wait for one (or more) of its famous crunch coffeecakes or mooncakes.
Other mouthwatering favorites you can choose from include dumplings,
custard buns, doughnuts, and fortune cookies.

. . . or discover a mural such as the one of Bruce Lee, who was born here in 1940
during his father's opera tour through the United States. His family returned
to Hong Kong, but at age 18, Bruce came back to San Francisco and became an actor.
His movies showcased his martial arts skills, and gained a large cult following
around the world.

The Bruce Lee mural is just one example of many unusual, beautiful,
intriguing murals found along the streets of Chinatown!

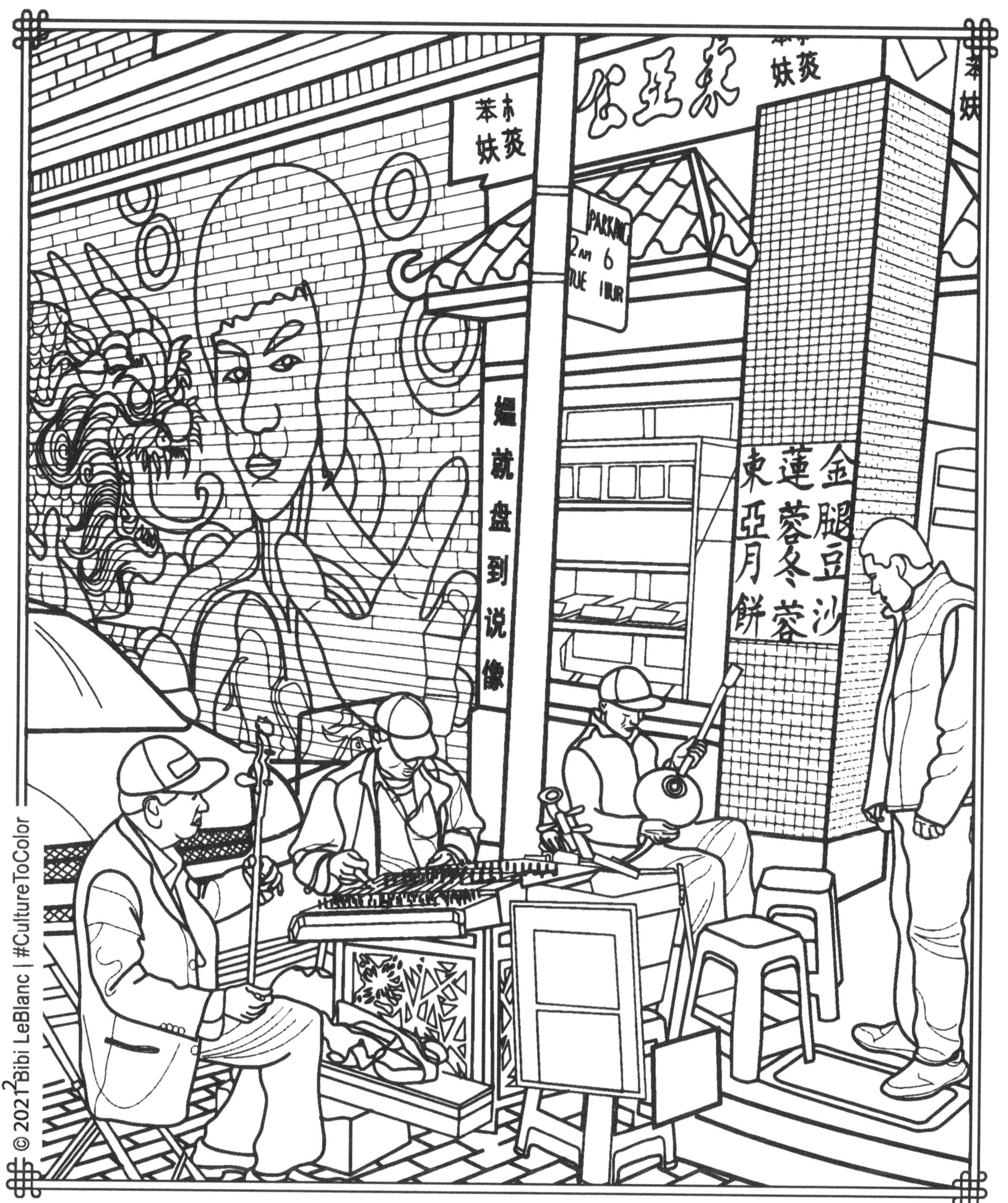

STREET LIFE

街头生活

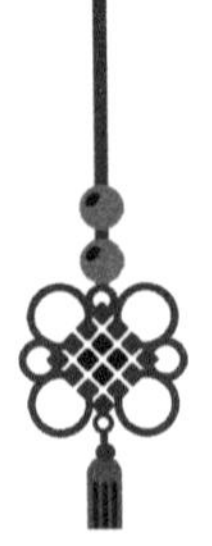

MAP OF CHINATOWN
中国城的地图

Bordered by Powell, Broadway, Kearny, and Bush, Chinatown is a city within San Francisco, covering 24 blocks or a 1.34-square-mile area.

Explore this iconic neighborhood with its many treasures, some easy to spot, some hidden away in small alleys.

HERE ARE A FEW SIGHTS TO GET YOU STARTED:

Dragon Gate

Sing Chong & Sing Fat Buildings

Old St. Mary's Cathedral

Portsmouth Square

Golden Gate Fortune Cookie Factory

East West Bank, aka Old Telephone Exchange

Chinese Historical Society of America

Willie "Woo Woo" Wong Playground

Nam Kue Chinese School

Clarion Performing Arts Center & Showgirl Magic Museum

Great Star Theater

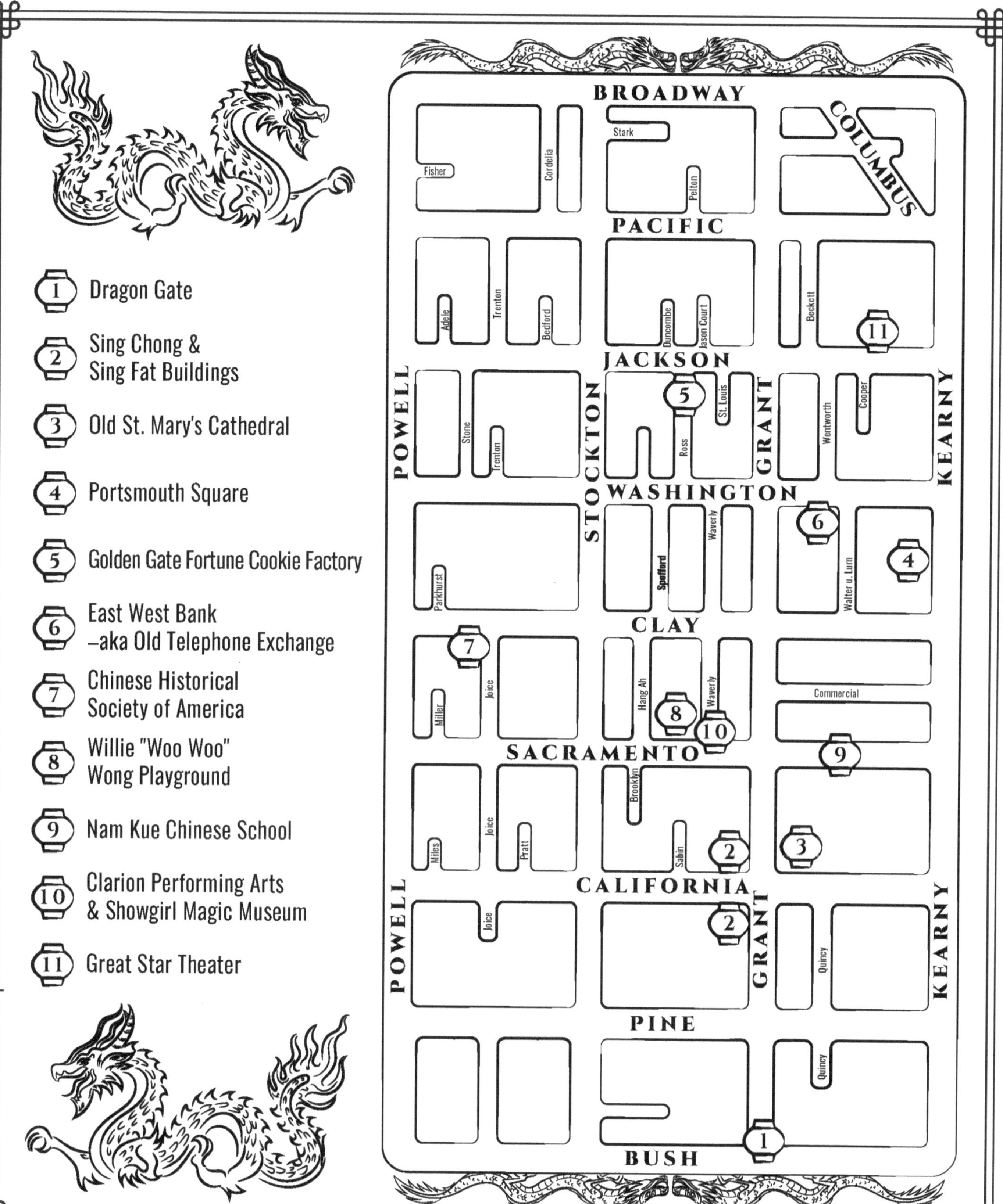

MAP OF CHINATOWN

中国城的地图

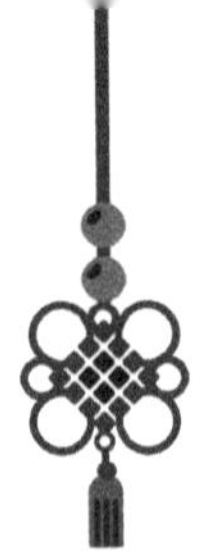

BLANK SCROLL
空白卷轴

What did you like best and enjoy most?

What inspired you during your visit to Chinatown?

Here's your chance to get creative!

We would love to see your creations.
Send photos or videos to Bibi@CultureToColor.com
or post on your social media with
#culturetocolor and #sfchinatown.

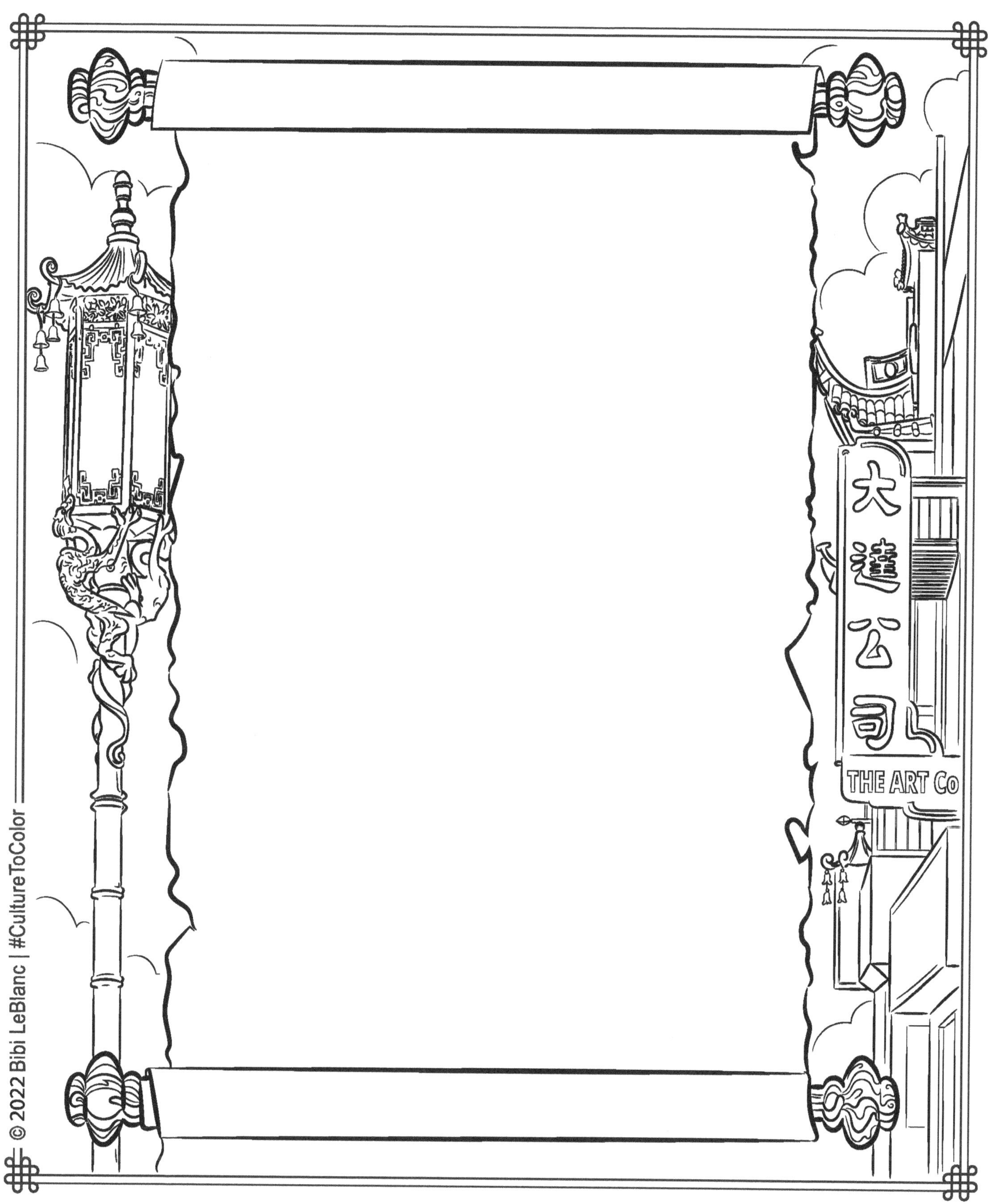

BLANK SCROLL

空白卷轴

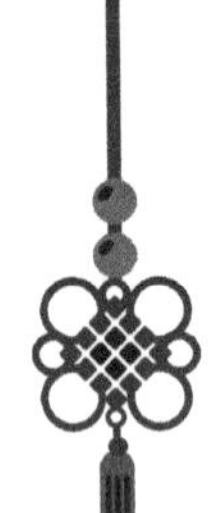

THANK YOU!

谢谢你

*"Music, food, and art bring people together
and create community."*
— Betty Louie

A special note of gratitude to Betty Louie and the Robert Louie Memorial Fund,*
whose generous support led to the creation of this book!

Thank you to the many people who unselfishly gave their time, shared their expertise,
and imparted their wisdom to help make this book a reality!

I am grateful for the new friends I made, the knowledge I gained during my research,
and the sense of community I experienced during my many visits to Chinatown!

Bibi

CULTURE TO COLOR

* The Robert Joseph Louie Memorial Fund is deeply involved in this community,
providing developmental and social programs for its residents.
The Fund is a proud advocate of Chinatown's history, culture, and traditions.

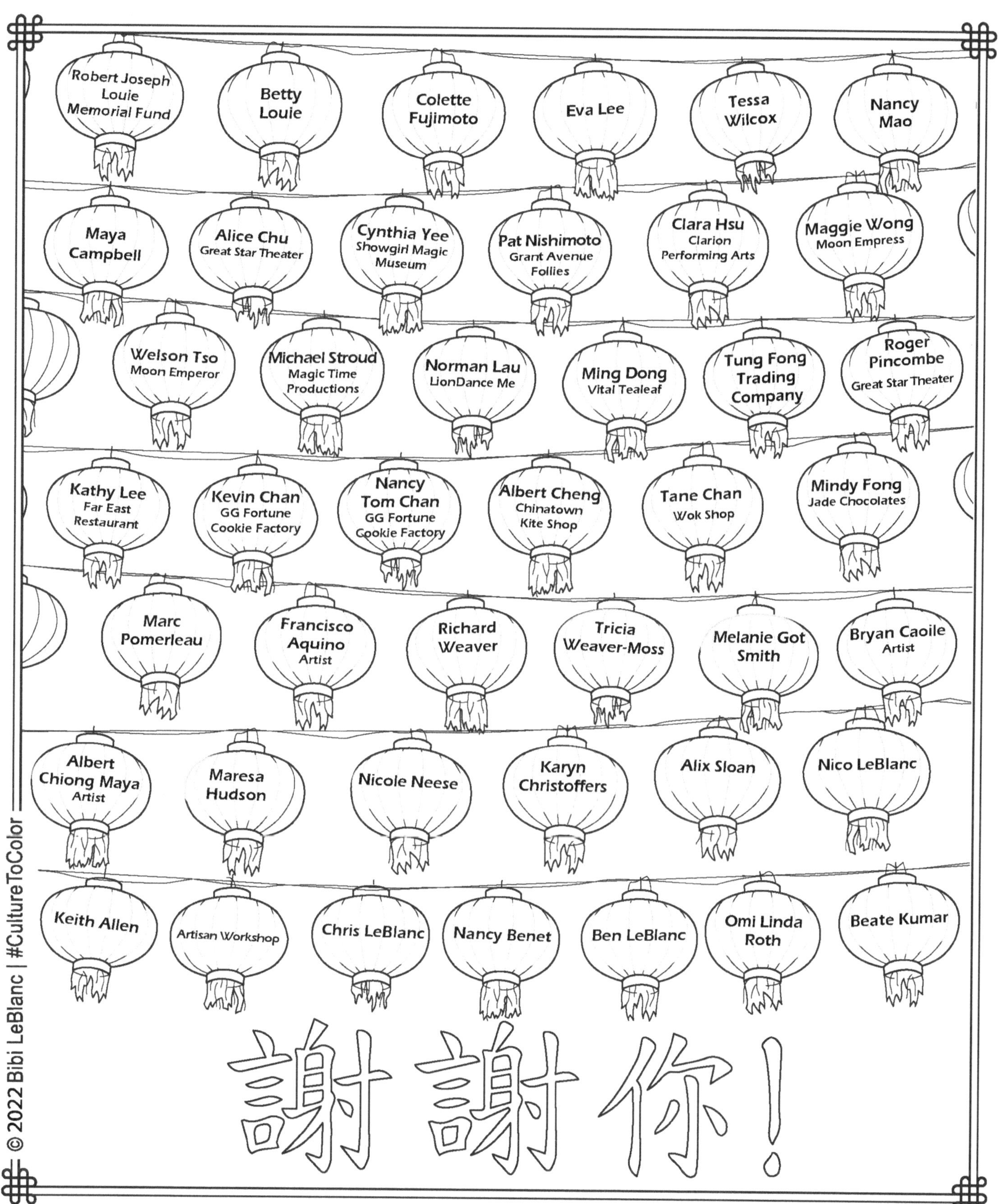

THANK YOU!

谢谢你

Resources

San Francisco Chinatown Visitor Information Center: bestofsfchinatown.com
San Francisco Chinatown: sanfranciscochinatown.com
Chinese Culture Center: cccsf.us
Chinese Historical Society of America: chsa.org
Chinatown Community Development Center: chinatowncdc.org
History of San Francisco Chinatown: history.com/topics/immigration/san-francisco-chinatown
Autumn Moon Festival: moonfestival.org
Bian Lian - Face Changing: magictimeproductions.com
Cable Cars: sfcablecar.com
Chinatown Restaurants: fareastcafesf.com
Chinese Chess
Chinese Kites: chinatownkite.com
Chinese New Year Parade: chineseparade.com
Clarion Performing Arts Center: theclarionsf.org
Dim Sum
Dragon Gate
Dragons & Dragon Dance
East West Bank – Former Chinese Telephone Exchange
Eastern Bakery: easternbakery.com
Fortune Cats
Golden Gate Fortune Cookie Factory: goldengatefortunecookies.com
Grant Avenue
Grant Avenue Follies: grantavenuefollies.com
Great Star Theater: greatstartheater.org
Herb Store
Jade Chocolates: jadechocolates.com
Lion Dance: liondanceme.com
Mahjong
Nam Kue Chinese School: nkssf.org
Old St. Mary's Cathedral & St. Mary's Square: oldsaintmarys.org
Portsmouth Square
Showgirl Magic Museum: theclarionsf.org/showgirl-magic-museum
Sing Fat & Sing Chong Buildings
Stockton Street Markets: bestofsfchinatown.com/destinations/stockton-street-market
Tai Chi
Tea: vitaltealeaf.net
Willie "Woo Woo" Wong Playground & Clubhouse: sfparksalliance.org/our-parks/parks/willie-woo-woo-wong-playground
Wok Shop: wokshop.com

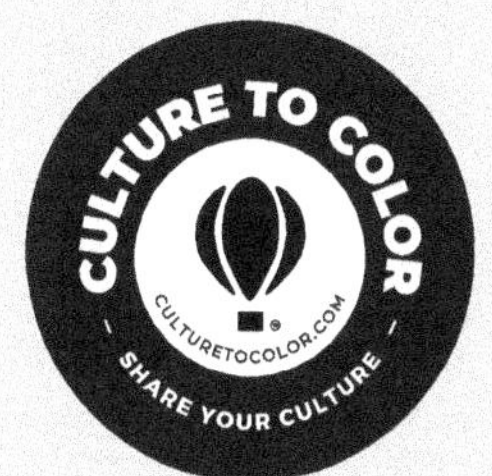

FOLLOW US ON:
Facebook: @CultureToColor
Twitter: @CultureColor
Instagram: @Culture_To_Color
YouTube: @CultureToColor
Pinterest: @CultureToColor
Tag us with your colored pages #culturetocolor

For more information visit:
www.CultureToColor.com

CONTACT:
Bibi LeBlanc
Culture to Color, LLC
cs@culturetocolor.com
USA: 386-228-5147

Titles available in the Culture to Color Series

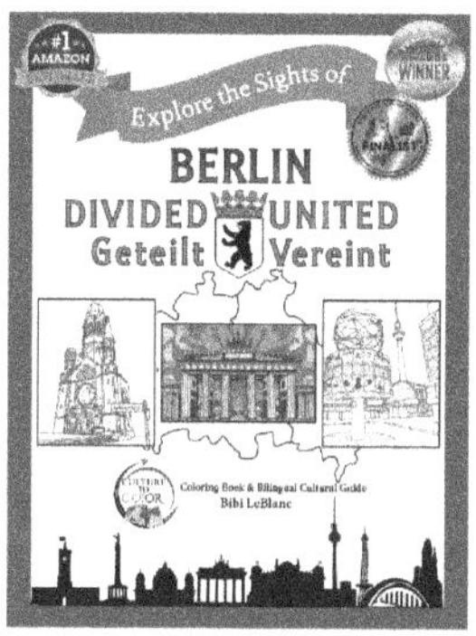
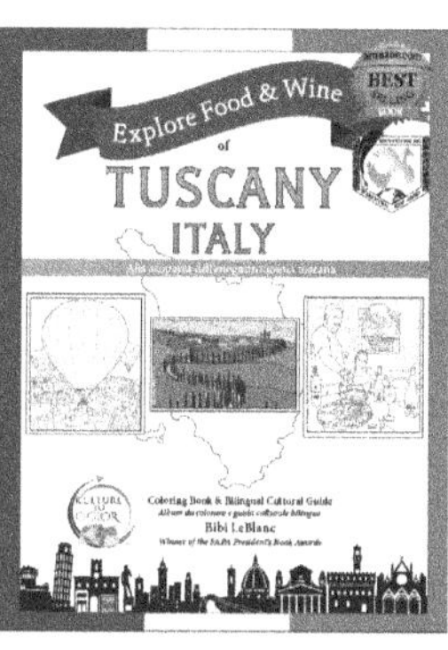
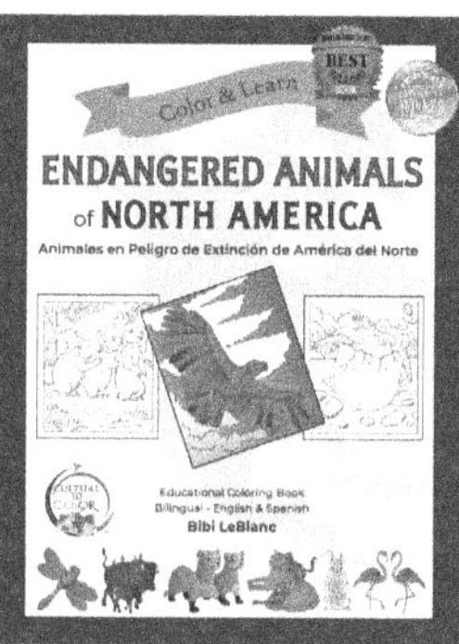
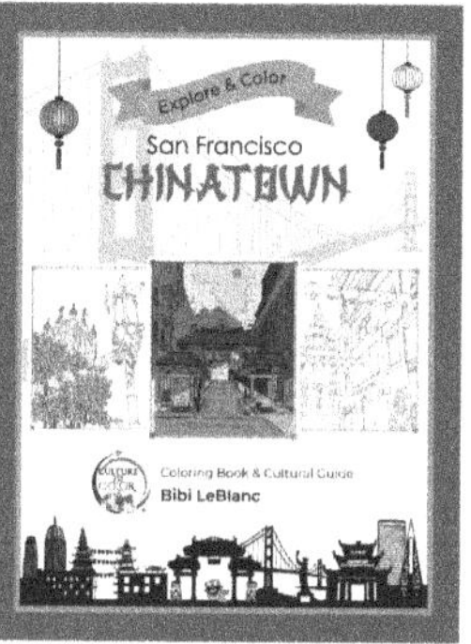

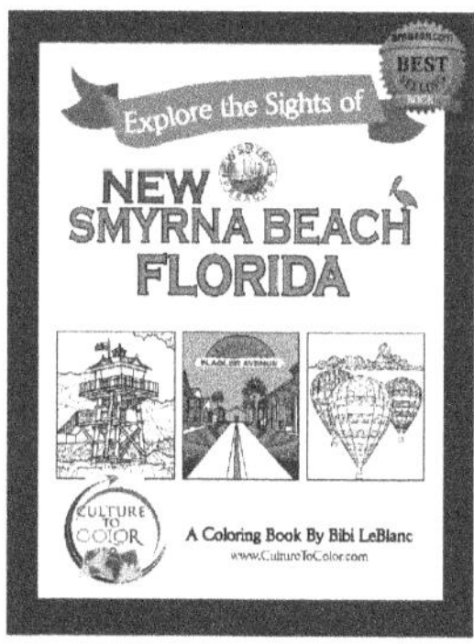
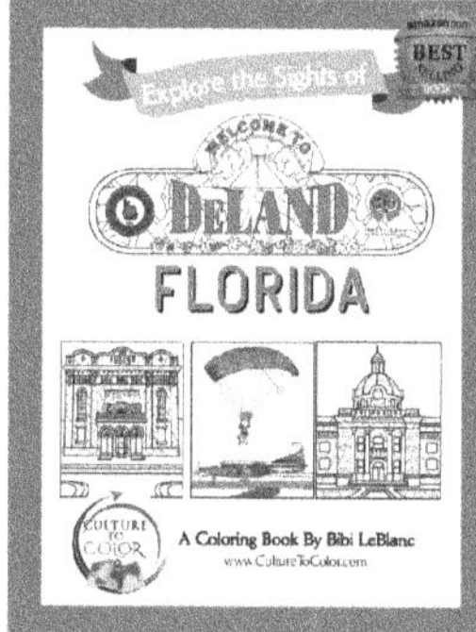
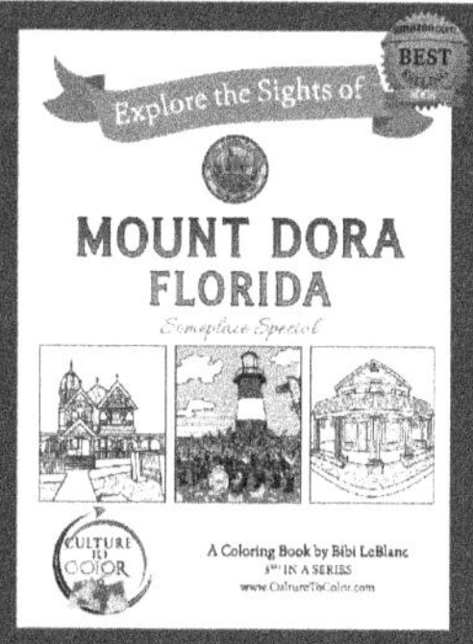
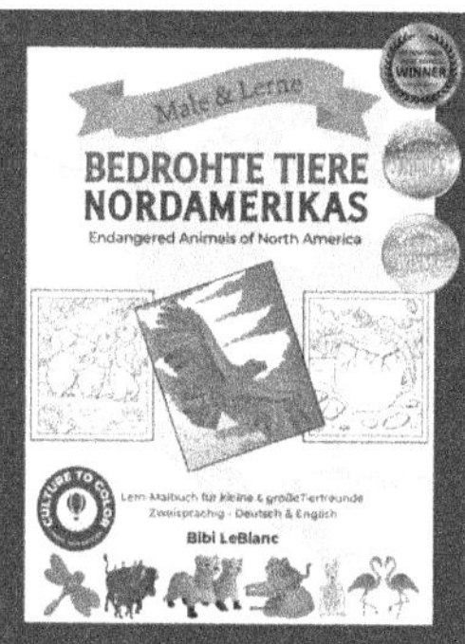

Titles available in the Culture to Color Wellness Series

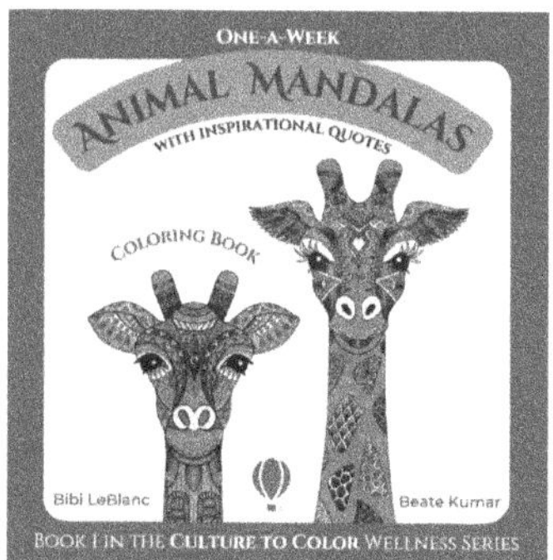
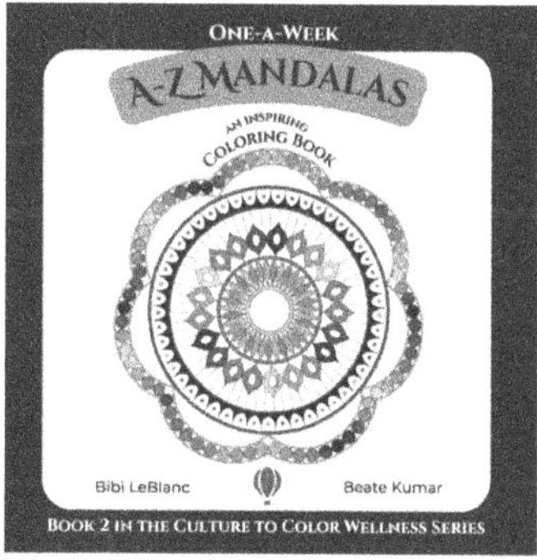
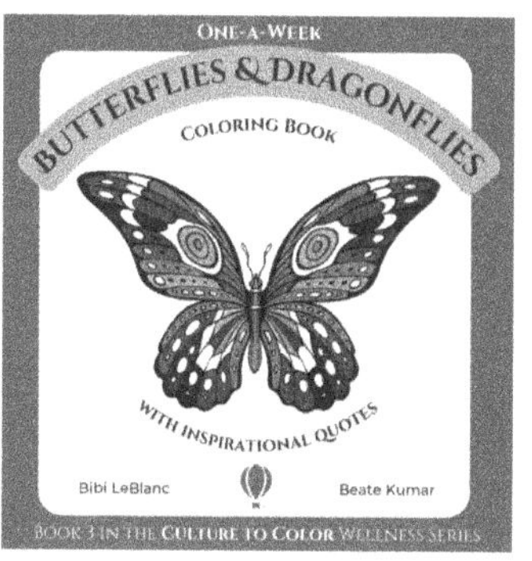

EVEN MORE COLORING ENJOYMENT LISTED ON THE NEXT PAGE . . .

Titles available in the Culture to Color Holiday Wellness Series

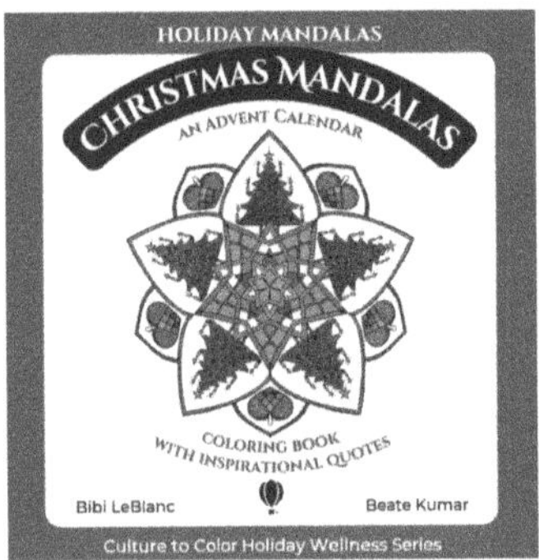

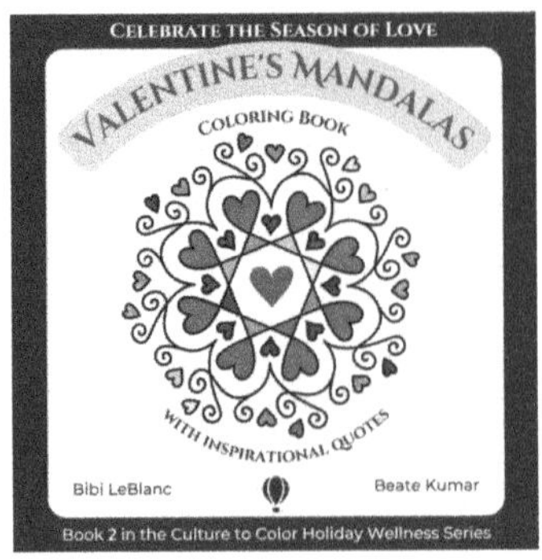